GOLD PANS AND IRON SKILLETS

Gold Pans
and
Iron Skillets

✤

CAROL M. GREEN

SEABOARD PRESS
JAMES A. ROCK & COMPANY, PUBLISHERS

Gold Pans and Iron Skillets, by Carol M. Green

SEABOARD PRESS

is an imprint of JAMES A. ROCK & CO., PUBLISHERS

Gold Pans and Iron Skillets copyright ©2008 by Carol M. Green

Special contents of this edition copyright ©2008 by Seaboard Press

All applicable copyrights and other rights reserved worldwide. No part of this publication may be reproduced, in any form or by any means, for any purpose, except as provided by the U.S. Copyright Law, without the express, written permission of the publisher.

Note: Product names, logos, brands, and other trademarks occurring or referred to within this work are the property of their respective trademark holders.

Page 6: *Doctrine and Covenants,* Published by the Church of Jesus Christ of Latter-Day Saints, Salt Lake City, UT 1989.

Address comments and inquiries to:
SEABOARD PRESS
9710 Traville Gateway Drive, #305
Rockville, MD 20850

E-Mail:
jrock@rockpublishing.com   lrock@rockpublishing.com
Internet URL: www.rockpublishing.com

Trade Paperback ISBN-13/EAN: 978-1-59663-626-2

Library of Congress Control Number: 2008920037

Printed in the United States of America

First Edition: 2008

To Wells

a.k.a. The Miner, Dad, and Pa

and to Esther

a.k.a. Mom

Thank you for providing
rich life experiences without
which there would have been no book

Acknowledgments

I express my gratitude to Lynne Rock, my Production Manager, for her guidance and patience throughout the editorial and production phase of this work.

To Roger, my very black, very deceased cat, you were an inspiration.

To Jonny, welcome to the family!

Special Thanks

To my husband, Kevin, who allows me the freedom to be who I am.

To my children Marie, Spencer, and Brock, whose need to know their heritage prompted the creation of this book.

To Ronda, my True Roommate, for her role as proofreader.

To James A. Rock & Co., Publishers, for taking a chance on an unknown author.

And to My Maker who granted me the gift of gab.

Contents

Foreword
    You'll Never Know Unless You Try xi

Preface xiii

CHAPTER ONE
The Early Years
    New Mexico Puffball Incident 3
    Never Go Skinny Dipping Without Your Panties! 4
    The Magic of Simple Things 6
    Winter Survival 10
    A Raggedy Christmas 13
    The Flood 15

CHAPTER TWO
Taste Therapy
    How to Clean a Trout 19
    How to Fry a Fish 21
    How to Bone a Fish 24
    If You Can Find It, You Can Eat It 26
    Can A Cookie Cure A Cold? 28
    Just Because You Can, Doesn't Mean You Should 30
    When All Else Fails, Bake 32

CHAPTER THREE
Felines and Feathers
    I Wish I Were a Cat 39
    And Then There Are Black Cats 41
    How to Slay a Rooster 44
    Egg Gathering and Chick Hatching 47
    Electric Fences 50

CHAPTER FOUR
Risky Recreation
    So You Want to Buy a Boat 57
    How to Water Ski 60
    How to Drop a Ski 64
    Camping We Will Go 66
    Rock Identification 69
    How to Pan for Gold 71
    No More Boat 74

CHAPTER FIVE
The Later Years
    My Search for Mr. Right 79
    Let the Games Begin 80
    Like Son, Like Father 82

CHAPTER SIX
Mom and Pa-isms
    Always Go Home with the Guy What Brung Ya 87
    To Forbid is to Motivate 90
    Oh, About So … 92
    Now, That's a Baby 94
    Keep a Candle Burning 97

Foreword

You'll Never Know Unless You Try

How is it that some folks are just blessed with wisdom? They don't require formal training to understand human nature. They don't display framed certificates verifying their qualifications to render advice, because they don't have them. Nor do they need them. They just have an inherent ability to assess a situation, consider the degree of seriousness it entails, weigh the consequences of various actions, and then determine the best path. So it was with my mother. Mom could calmly view what I thought to be tragic circumstances and then help steer me in the right direction. It didn't require a lengthy discussion to convey her advice. A simple statement usually did the trick. One of the best pieces of advice she ever gave was, "You'll never know unless you try."

In the spring of my sixth grade year of school, I had been encouraged by my peers to run for the very important office of seventh grade cheerleader. I was new at this particular school, and as the election was determined by popular vote, I concluded that I had not been in my new school long enough to establish myself as *popular* and therefore had no chance of success. Upon relating these thoughts to my mother, she simply said, "You'll never know unless you try." Well, I wanted to know. So, I tried. And then, I knew.

I have used this advice with my own children and they have realized success in their efforts. When they feel inadequate in the classroom, behind a microphone, or on the playing field, they know that it is expected of them to try—to give it their best effort. That is all that is required. They can walk away knowing that they did their best.

The opportunity to try continues to present itself throughout my life. Mom's words have echoed in my mind through the years. When faced with a new and often intimidating challenge, my curiosity often overcomes my fear. My desire to *know* urges me onward. This is not to say that my need to know has been irrational. I am a firm believer in the old adage, "curiosity killed the cat," but when a lack of confidence threatens to restrain my efforts, Mom's words come back to me and cheer me on. What I *know* is that I have not always been successful, but that I have attempted to achieve, and therein lies the accomplishment.

So it is with this book. I have long desired to publish a work of value. I have long imagined myself a successful author. I have not *known* whether I could achieve such a goal, but Mom's words continue to move me toward my target and my desire to *know* is the reason I must *try*.

This work is intended to teach and entertain. If the reader learns little from the pages of this book, I would pray that he absorbs one thing—that is to *try*. Give it his best effort. The value of an endeavor does not always lie in its outcome. Often true worth is gained by the experience—the increase in knowledge gained along the way. And, if the reader doesn't enjoy a laugh or two, I would be sorely disappointed, for life should be full of laughter as mine certainly has been.

Preface

My parents raised seven children, the first arriving during World War II. Recovering one's dreams after the war was difficult and though they didn't always provide monetary riches, the life lessons they taught were invaluable. Dad could do anything — farming, building, mining for gold, and telling jokes. Mom could make a meal out of seemingly nothing, she could construct and later remodel an evening gown from scratch, and now eighty-four-years-old, she still gives good advice. It is this heritage that inspired *Gold Pans and Iron Skillets*.

Gold Pans and Iron Skillets is a collection of life lessons presented in a humorous, yet practical form. There are three main themes throughout this work. 1) Life is not as complicated as most folks believe. Teaching frugality is as simple as boning a fish. 2) There is a lesson in every experience. Often the journey is more valuable than the outcome. 3) One can find humor in any situation. A sense of humor may very well save one's sanity

CHAPTER ONE

The Early Years

New Mexico Puffball Incident

My childhood was crowded with adventures, many of them real, some imagined. To the impressionable young mind of a five-year-old, even threatened adventures can be horrific. So it was with the New Mexico Puffball Incident.

Giant Puffball Mushrooms, technically known as *Lycoperdon Maximum*, can appear extremely menacing to a youngster upon first encounter. One particular puffball was discovered alone in a grassy field in the hills of New Mexico. The Miner Forty-niner, a.k.a. Wells, had taken his youngest girls and their mother on yet another adventure, mining Mica and Amazonite with the assistance of some New Mexico Natives and a few sticks of dynamite. On one damp morning the Giant Puffball was discovered. The Miner declared that Esther would be fixing this tasty dish for dinner. After all, we *were* living off the land. The idea did not seem too incredible as we were also residing in a pickup and camper, bathing in ponds and making imaginary motorcycles out of old tree stumps. Never having encountered a puffball, I was somewhat apprehensive. It resembled a batch of bread dough, minus the bowl and warm yeasty scent. I still associate the aroma of damp milkweed with bulging puffballs—and danger!

Esther, ever ready to play along, ceremoniously presented the monstrous mushroom on a large dinner plate. I was certain my parents were going to make me bite into that thing! Only when the knife was inserted and a triangle slice removed was I certain they could not force me to take a bite! The interior was dark olive green goo. Disgusting! It was so disgusting that my younger and older siblings have both blocked the experience from their memories. Esther denies it. Wells is no longer here to argue about it. But *I* know there was a puffball with a knife in it on a plate in a camper in New Mexico!

Lycoperdon Maximum. It is edible while yet unripe. It can grow to nearly 20 inches in diameter. Ominous! When ripe the flesh turns green, flaccid, and mushy. Odor and flavor become, yes, disgusting! As it continues to age, the green flesh dries and becomes a dark powdery sponge that escapes its skin, scattering spores to give life to yet more puffballs. If conditions are right—humidity and temperature allowing—additional ominous edible mushrooms may appear.

Now I knew I didn't like the looks of the thing when I first saw it. The Miner's threat of consumption made it even more disagreeable; and on closer inspection, it was apparent that I would forgo the edible experience—at all costs! Fortunately, it wasn't necessary that I snub my proper upbringing by refusing to clean up my plate—another sign of danger. The Giant Puffball itself saved me. Its hideous flesh had the last laugh, for neither of my prankster parents could bring themselves to partake of that green gooey surprise!

Never Go Skinny Dipping Without Your Panties!

New Mexico was an adventure, on so many levels! Though living in the hills in a camper may be inconvenient and uncomfortable for some, it was simply a way of life for two little girls. The thirteen-year-old, however, had a much more difficult existence. While three and five-year-olds can fit in a wash tub and, therefore, have nearly the same bathing experience as they would at home, an older child cannot fully submerge herself in a fifteen gallon container.

So it happened that we found ourselves having a swim in a secluded pond, accompanied by a bar of soap and a few fish. Through history there have been occasions when the younger siblings proved wiser and more prepared than their elders as in the cases of Nephi, Abel, and Joseph of Egypt. History repeats itself.

The thirteen-year-old (she will remain nameless to protect her pride) was so happy to have a complete bathing experience that she embraced the opportunity with full abandon of clothing. The younger, more skeptical, and more reserved girls refused to remove their undergarments in case of an emergency. After all, their panties would dry.

It felt good, though cold, to be splashing and paddling in abundant water. Unfortunately, the secluded pond was not nearly as private as had heretofore been assumed. Whilst in the middle of lathering her long awaited shampoo job, the thirteen-year-old was surprised, even alarmed to hear what most certainly was a shotgun fired! Fearing that she had been mistaken for a deer, white tailed of course, she frantically submerged herself in the cold pond water hoping to rinse her hair and hold her breath long enough for the hunters to pass. The younger girls crossed their arms over their naked chests and began scrambling out of the water to find their clothing, thankful that they were wearing panties.

Presently, a pickup full of yelling, laughing New Mexico Natives passed by on a dirt road. The thirteen-year-old nearly collapsed. Grateful that she wasn't the mistaken target of a deer hunt, she donned her clothing and returned to the camp of her father. To her dismay, she discovered the pickup full of yelling, laughing New Mexico Natives had arrived before her and were actually her father's acquaintances! Face ashen, she hid herself amongst some sagebrush until the *hunters* departed.

The younger girls, smug in their wisdom to retain coverage of their hind parts, went about their business, suffering no lingering consequences. The thirteen-year-old, however, still endures emotional pain and scarring. Her sisters feel for her, yet they are certain her ailments could have been avoided had she only worn her panties!

Hint: *Doctrine and Covenants*, 38:30 "… if ye are prepared ye shall not fear."

The Magic of Simple Things

What ever happened to make believe? Does anyone own simple toys or play group games that involve only a ball or a couple of rules? *Everybody* owns a video game or an iPod. One would rather be entertained than create entertainment. One could save a great deal of money if he took a page out of yesterday's playbook.

Make believe. Technology has created an entire world of entertainment so realistic it is sometimes difficult to remember the joy of the imagination or the lack of limitations when a child sets his creative mind in gear. I had a make believe motorcycle. It was an old tree stump found in the hills of New Mexico. Its roots were my handles—its bark, a custom paint job. I could give my younger sister rides all over the countryside on my motor bike. My son had a make believe motorcycle, as well. His was the truly imaginary kind. No props. It existed only in his mind

... and in our ears! In imaginary mode he would ride his bike around the house increasing the drone of the rpm's as he prepared to shift gears. He never broke form, nor acknowledged our existence. It was the most inexpensive toy we've ever owned!

Tree horses (it's not a typo) were created by peeling the bark off leaning poplar trees (I'm sure the trees were already dead), straddling the trunk, and bouncing up and down. Those were some long skinny horses! Ever obedient, they took us wherever our imagination allowed. Rock houses come in many shapes, but their size is only extra large. My favorites were found in Targhee National Forest. Granite boulders the size of large automobiles provided hours of entertainment as we *claimed* possession of various rocks to serve as bedrooms and living spaces. My children don't quite understand when I exclaim, "Oh, look, a house rock!" However, they have found, as did I, a more readily available *house* in the removable cushions of the family sofa. Smaller in area, they too provide a boundary of sorts to afford a young imagination her own space. Haystacks supplied the materials for a make believe domain, as well as a literal home for cats and mice!

Simple toys. Endroll paper (that's what we called it) was leftover newsprint that wouldn't last through one printing. It was one of my favorite toys as a child. The Miner would randomly bring home the prized item, and two little girls would presently go about fashioning life size paper dolls. The dolls were traced and cut from the large roll ends, then colored to match each of the girls' hair color, eyes, and favorite article of clothing. If an ankle was too thin or a hand was mistakenly cut off, the procedure would begin again, granting Esther hours of quiet as we worked diligently at our task. When completed, the *paper* girls would rest elegantly on the living room sofa, waiting for someone to notice that they were not live girls. When the life size creations grew tiresome, paper chains of smaller dolls could be cut and strewn on the basement floor. Snowflakes, paper airplanes, and doll house diagrams were also created from the magical rolls.

Colored chalk not only decorated the endroll paper, it also created hopscotch grids and traffic signs on the sidewalk to be used in the game of *Cops and Robbers*. *Cops and Robbers* required bicycles, neighbor boys, and backyard hideouts. Many a nightgown or embroidered dish towel was ruined while serving as a chalk eraser!

A roll of string stretched a long way in providing entertainment. Over the ear, under the nose, over the other ear, and pull! Now giggle. Tin can stilts and paper cup telephones could be fashioned with the aid of a good piece of string. Cat's Cradle provided hours of entertainment, confusion, and knot undoing!

Any number of uses could be found for a Frisbee, a jump rope, or an abandoned inner tube. The Frisbee, intended for a game of catch, often acted as a serving tray, base marker for a game of kickball, or dress up hat brim. Jump ropes used individually or with a group, served as cat leashes, fashion belts, or handcuffs during the *Cops and Robbers* era. Every child needs inner tubes. They come in handy (and we won't tell the protective folks) in irrigation ditches, swimming pools, and settling ponds. They suffice as a lawn chair or recliner during a game of *house*. One can become dizzy enough to be sick when he is tucked inside and rolled along the grass.

Jacks, marbles, and crayons, though different in design and purpose tend to end up in the same boat, or shoebox. They never remain in the original container. This is evidenced by scrutinizing the contents of any given *junk drawer* on any given day. One will inevitably discover lost marbles, broken crayons, and stray jacks. Why these items reside in the *junk drawer* is ever a mystery. They should be in the very nice, worn out shoe box or empty soup can provided for them.

Probably the most ingenious of the simple toys of my youth was the homemade waterslide, predecessor to the current Wham-o Slip "n" Slide. Wells, The Miner, prepared a strip of conveyor belt from a potato harvester. It was placed on a slight incline in the yard. A water hose was positioned near the top of the belt. There was just enough room between the slide and the house to get a little run and then dive belly flop style onto the belt careening the length thereof. The neighborhood children all turned out for this grand event. Hours of fun ensued until the neighborhood Chow joined the fun. Wet dog fur took some of the joy out of the game. The blackened clothing often went the way of improvised chalk erasers!

Games. Something unique about group games is that they often appeal to young and old alike. The aged may adopt the role of tutor, only to become immersed in the fun. The young make up for their inexperience with enthusiasm and energy. The games of the past are becoming lost amongst the games of the computer. Leap Frog, Mother May I, Red Rover, Any Eye Over, and Button Button, are foreign games to the youth of the present. I don't know if I remember the rules!

The most magical toys however, happened to be those that were dangerous and delightful. The danger often supplying the delight! The Frog Pond, which was actually any body of water containing tadpoles or pollywogs, served as a muddy, messy source of entertainment. Imagine, catching one's own baby critters and watching them lose their tails and grow their legs as they mature into adults! Then the sorrow as the expired reptiles were steamed in the sun or dehydrated in their forgotten containers. Abandoned barns with rotting timbers, irrigation ditches—empty or full, fallen trees and old farm equipment, all were potential hazards, yet they allowed the imagination to stretch. Chasing the ABC buses (Correction: *AEC* for Atomic Energy Commission) just to hear the driver pull the air horn and watch the passengers wave was an evening ritual that no conscionable parent would allow today. What if those men were violent? What if that bus driver didn't see the children? What if … ?

Must one forever be entertained? Must one live life without risks? Might he experience life more fully if he engages his creative talents and imagines how high he can soar, how deep he can dig with nothing but a common dinner spoon, how fast he can drive, or how far he can slide? Call me boring and old fashioned. Call me technologically challenged. Call me on a land line!

Winter Survival

Winter survival is not just a Boy Scout Merit Badge. It is a fact of life that long winters must be dealt with. There are a number of ways to do this ranging from hibernation to leaving the country. Neither of these options is very practical as one is not a bear, nor can the entire northern half of the country reside in Arizona. Suggestion? Don't beat winter, enjoy it!

In the land of the Rocky Mountains in the winter there are two things a little girls needs—a pair of ice skates and a pair of snow boots. Oh, and quite possibly a couple of bread sacks to slip over her shoes enabling them to slide into her rubber snow boots. Those were the days!

Water does freeze and remain frozen long enough for outdoor ice skating entertainment. This can be done on a designated ice rink provided by flooding a vacant lot, or by skating on the frozen water remaining in the local irrigation canal, and sometimes on the street if the snow has been packed hard enough! First, one must don a coat, hat and mittens, then pull the bread sacks over her shoes, and stomp them into her snow boots. Then sling a pair of ice skates over her shoulder and brace to face the bitter cold outdoors.

If she is fortunate the trek to the ice rink will be short as her nostrils begin to stick together shortly after venturing outside. Upon reaching the rink she must locate a seat, usually a log or rock, on which to perch while removing her gloves, snow boots, bread sacks, and shoes. Then she must untie the knot joining her ice skate strings together. At this point she may need to pause to insert fingers into her mouth in order to thaw them enough to maintain dexterity. Inserting foot into ice skate, she then laces her skate and secures it with a bow. Again, she pauses for finger thawing then puts on the second skate. After skates are secured she quickly inserts her hands into mittens and puts her shoes and sacks into boots for safekeeping.

It is now time to enjoy the ice. Wobbling carefully onto the rink she soon finds herself caught up in the flow of skating traffic. So long as she remains upright and those around her do the same, she will continue to move in a counter clockwise direction, enjoying the glide of her skate blades across the ice. However, as with any forward moving traffic, there is inevitably a crash. It may be self inflicted or the result of another's mishap, but the fall will come. If lucky, her feet will come out from under her and she will land on the padded most part of herself. Otherwise, her hands and knees will be the first to make contact with the ice, causing excruciating pain! She will pause to inspect the ice for indentations and cracks before returning to a standing position. When the joy has been had and she can no longer feel the pain of cold in her fingers and toes, it is time to return home. She must first remove her skates.

She removes her mittens as finger thawing must once again take place. It is not as effective as prior to skating for the girl is anxious to get home, and her fingers are much more frozen. Hopefully, she did not tie her skate strings too securely. She unlaces her skates and pries them from her frosty feet. Now, she must insert same feet into chilly shoes, bread sacks, and rubber boots. This process takes much longer than it did indoors prior to her skating venture. Her hands are cold. Her feet are cold. Her shoes, sacks, and boots are cold, thus refusing to slip easily into place. She attempts to tie her skate strings together, but aborts the effort as her fingers are now curled into a scratching claw-like position. She slowly pulls on her mittens, tucks an ice skate under each elbow, and trudges home.

Upon returning home the girl removes all of her outerwear and drops it conveniently just inside the front door where it warms and pools thawed ice all over the floor. Nose running, fingers stinging, and cheeks aflame, she heads immediately to the kitchen sink where someone has convinced her that running her fingers under *cold* water will warm them. When she can stand it no longer, she dries her hands, as best she can given the fact that they are not very cooperative, and proceeds to find some quiet indoor activity such as a nap.

Similar procedures (minus the skates) are required for snowman building, snow fort construction, and snowball fights. The outdoor gear must be donned and the thawing process occurs after the fun has been had.

What value this outdoor activity? Exercise, fresh air, sunshine, all of which are key to a healthy, happy existence. Esther swears that the winters she sent her children outside to play each day, they never experienced colds or flu. We justify our season ski passes as part of our overall health regimen. (Too bad the IRS doesn't see it that way.) And it works. We are happier and healthier because we *get out in it*. Don't ignore the cold. Don't fight it. Embrace it. Experience it. Enjoy it. And send me the money saved on doctor visits. (No reimbursements for accidental health care!)

A Raggedy Christmas

It must have been about 1966, for I recall that I was not yet in school. The memories remain, few but vivid. I remember a sewing machine, bits of fabric, a door that remained closed, sneaking a peek with my younger sister and straining to decipher the whispers coming from behind the door. For two small girls, the expectations were wonderful. Our excitement was limited only by our imaginations! Whatever could be happening in that room?

The secret emerged Christmas morning. Beneath our tree sat two of the largest, happiest, rag dolls we had ever seen. Raggedy Ann and Raggedy Andy! At least, they were almost the Raggedys. The dolls were twenty-four inches tall, with orange (not red) hair, red triangle noses, wide spaced black button eyes, and red boots that pointed East and West. They were identical. The only distinguishing characteristic was their clothing. Andy looked like a clown in his one-piece suit and pointed hat. His striped suit was ruffled at the wrists and ankles. It had a red ruffled collar. Ann's dress had a blue bodice and a dark print skirt with an apron attached. A pocket on her apron housed a bright red hankie. Ann wore a scarf that complimented Andy's clown suit. I remember most the buttons down each back: three candy-colored buttons that looked like great big Life Savers. They were a comical pair. Situated under the tree atop a pile of packages, Ann and Andy appeared to be two children, the first to arise on Christmas Morn already wise to the contents of their brightly colored perch.

I found Raggedy Ann the other day, not in a trunk in an attic where any self-respecting Raggedy Ann would be found, but in a foot locker in the garage amongst old school books, a cheerleader's uniform, and some old birthday cards. Raggedy Ann was in sad shape! She was hairless. Her skirt was torn and her scarf and hankie were missing. Her black button eyes were merely glue spots. Worst of all, she was decapitated! It appeared that Raggedy Ann had endured far too many visits from my nieces and nephews. I contemplated laying Ann in her final resting place (the wastebasket), but thought better of it. I would attempt to revive her!

This time it was my sewing machine, my fabric, and my wide-eyed five-year-old daughter anticipating the treasure being created. As I traced the tattered fabric of Ann's body, I wondered what memories this renewed doll might sow for my little girl. Would she appreciate this silly looking creature as I did? Or, would Raggedy Ann be lost in the blur of Mom's many other projects? After all, she was just another doll wearing an old leftover dress.

To me, she is still Raggedy Ann. What makes her Raggedy is not the fabric, or the color of her hair, or the stuffing inside, but the memories of a little girl's Christmas captured by the expression on the doll's silly face. Each time I look at Raggedy Ann, I am reminded of a Christmas and a childhood filled with happiness. And now, each Christmas my renewed doll takes a seat of respect beneath my tree to remind me that Christmas is for children, for love, and for memories of long, long, ago when a child was born to bring love to all children. Raggedy Ann has become my reminder at Christmas and every other day. She is a symbol of love, of gifts, of joy, and of what Christmas is all about.

The Flood

You've heard the adage, "If you love something, set it free. If it comes back to you it's yours forever. If it doesn't come back, it was never yours in the first place." Well, at our house, it went something more like this, "If you love something, look for it. If you can't find it, it may have been lost in the flood."

There was a flood, and several moves, and self-appointed disposers of old and infrequently used items. However; it was most easy to blame the flood. Flood waters are not respecters of persons. They don't make way for the important, the ill, or the kind. Flood waters flow where they may. It is easy to personify flood waters, granting them evil characteristics, and blaming them for loss. Flood waters are dirty and even years later, leave a lasting stench and stain to those things in which they have come in contact. Food, clothing, stuffed toys, bedding, and carpet are better discarded than refurbished having been affected by flood waters. Four feet of dirty water in a basement is not catastrophic, but it leaves a long impression. So, began the excuse, "It must have been lost in the flood."

The excuse was valid at first. Jars and jars of preserves were dumped. Clothing was washed and eventually discarded as it wouldn't come completely clean. Stuffed toys were ruined. The basement, once an inviting place to play, became a smelly reminder of things that were gone. "Whatever happened to that old record player?" drew the response, "It was lost in the flood." "Do we have any more of that ..." received, "Nope. It was lost in the flood." My favorite doll—lost in the flood. Those old storybooks—flood. An antique dresser—the flood got it.

The Flood was a great culprit. How could one argue with the ravages of *The Flood?* Its victims had to be cast aside and replaced with new, less loved items. It was easier to blame *The*

Flood than to search for a missing item. Cleaning activities occur over the years. A move will necessitate the scaling down of one's belongings, if for no other reason than to simplify the packing process. Some families have kleptomaniacs. Others have throw-away-maniacs. Some of us are just forgetful. *The Flood* is always a good scapegoat. It happened over 35 years ago, but *The Flood* still gets blamed for things long gone; things lost, stolen, misplaced, or simply worn out. Who can argue with *The Flood?* If *The Flood* got it, who wants it back?

Give it a try next time you need an excuse. Break a toy? Blame it on *The Flood.* Lose your glasses? Blame it on *The Flood.* Hoarding all the family photos? Blame it on *The Flood.* Hiding ancient Native American artifacts? Blame it on *The Flood.* Break a jar of jam? Blame it on *The Flood.* Can't remember whose name you have for Christmas? Yep, blame it on *The Flood!*

Eat of the forbidden fruit? Blame it on the snake!

CHAPTER TWO

Taste Therapy

How to Clean a Trout

I learned at a very young age that there are certain life skills a young lady must develop. Some of them require more talent than others.

My father was a fisherman. As was his father. My mother was a fisherwoman and I became one, too. It doesn't do one much good to catch a fish to eat if one does not know the proper preparation techniques. The following steps must be done properly, and in order.

Step One: Removal of Fishhook

This should be done firmly and with confidence so as not to impale one's finger on said fishhook. Firmly grip the fish by the gills with thumb and index finger of left hand. (Yes, it does feel a little funny and the gills are a bit rough inside.) Grasp a pair of needle nose pliers in your right hand and secure the fishhook in the nose of the pliers. Here is where the confidence comes into play. Twist the pliers in a motion to allow the hook to *back out* of the fish mouth. (Yes, the fish is probably still alive and will writhe trying to free his gills from fisherman's grasp.) (Yes, he is a little slippery.) Remember confidence. *You are the fisherman!* Do not get excited. Do not impale one's finger on fishhook. Do not drop fish into river. Place flopping fish into fishing creel, small cooler, or Wal-Mart shopping bag, whichever is available. This is important if you intend to follow directions in the later chapter *How to Fry a Fish*.

When you have gathered your nerves, bandaged your impaled finger, and located a pocket knife, you may proceed to Step Two.

Step Two: Removal of Entrails

This step can be performed immediately after removal of hook or sometime after bandaging of finger, preferably within a few short hours. Again, confidence and deliberation are necessary for success.

Grasp fish along top of back in left hand. Turn wrist and expose soft white underbelly of trout. You will note a small dark spot near tail. It may be oozing, especially if you have been extremely firm in handling of fish! Hold pocketknife in right hand and insert tip into oozing cavity. Locate mouth of fish. Head for it with your knife taking care to slice through only the soft white outer tissue. This is similar to slicing open plastic wrapper on brick of cheese. Be careful not to puncture fish entrails. This will complicate removal! When knife tip arrives at base of fish's chin (He doesn't really have a chin. Just stop where his chin would be if he were to have one), remove knife and insert tip along fish jaw, relieving white skin along entire jaw. Once again holding fish by gills with thumb and forefinger of left hand, stick your right forefinger under jawbone and down fish's throat! Do not impale one's finger on fishhook left by skipping Step One. With firmness and conviction, pull entrails from mouth to oozing spot through opening created with knife tip. Throw entrails back into lake or stream, or drop into extra Wal-Mart shopping bag.

Step Three: Stop Gagging!

Step Four: Washing of Trout

Once again, grasp fish along top of back with left hand. He will still be slippery, but should not fight as he is most certainly dead if you followed Step Two properly. With right hand in marble shooting position run right thumb along inside of fish spine, thus removing any remaining entrails. Rinse fish well in lake, creek, or stream from garden hose. Please refrain from using kitchen sink. If you fail to hold him firmly, fish may appear to swim away in lake or stream. Remember, he is dead. You just lost a perfectly good dead fish.

Step Five: Keeping Fish Cold

Fish are meat. They must be kept cold prior to cooking. Place freshly cleaned fish in ice cold cooler, refrigerator, or freeze in container of water until ready to fry. Hint: Frozen fish must be thawed before cooking.

Step Six: Congratulate Yourself

You have just completed one of life's basic skills, properly, and in order. Unless, of course, you impaled your finger, punctured entrails, or let your dead fish swim away from you. Fortunately, this life lesson can be practiced until perfected. There will be other fish to clean.

How to Fry a Fish

If one is determined to consume fish, and he should be as it has been proven a very healthy form of protein, it is imperative that the fish be prepared to satisfaction. Having been a partaker of fish flesh from a very young age, it is essential that fish tastes like fish, and looks like fish! A *mild* fish is considered inadequate as it lessens the overall experience.

Step One: Clean the Fish

This should be accomplished following instructions in *How to Clean a Trout*. If one is a novice, it may be advisable to complete this task sometime prior to cooking and partaking of said fish. This time lapse will allow for recovery of *How to Clean a Trout—Step Three*. Do not dwell on hideousness of raw fish as prepared fish will prove delectable upon consumption.

Step Two: Obtain an Iron Skillet

Proper cooking utensils include a pancake turner, an iron skillet, and a heat source. The skillet must be large enough to contain chosen fish. A well-used skillet is preferred as its smooth patina will offer a non-stick surface requiring less cooking fat, thus supporting the theory that fish is healthy. The heat source may be a stove top, propane cooking unit, or campfire. If using a campfire, some skill in temperature regulation will be required.

Step Three: Prepare Cooking Supplies

Flour, salt, pepper, and some type of cooking fat will be required. In a low dish such as a pie tin, combine some flour with a dash or two of salt and a little pepper. Set aside. Cooking fat may be oil, butter, shortening, or bacon grease, whichever is available and/or preferred. Obviously, the bacon grease will contribute to flavor enhancement!

Step Four: Apply Heat

Place a dab of cooking fat in iron skillet and position skillet over heat source.

Step Five: Season Fish

Optimum fish length should be small enough to fit within skillet or approximately nine inches from mouth to tail. Yes, these should remain intact. (See *How to Bone a Fish*) Do not look fish in the eye as one may experience a small twinge of guilt. Toss fish in seasoned flour mixture. Be sure to coat entire fish—inside and out. Place reverently in heated pan.

Step Six: Flip Fish

Skin will begin to brown. Cook on one side until skin is crisp and eye begins to bulge. When floured fish skin is golden, gently work pancake turner between skillet and fish. When confident, raise fish from pan and tenderly invert fish and drop into pan. Additional cooking fat may be required at this time.

Step Seven: Finish Frying

Continue cooking until both eyes begin to bulge, skin and tail are crisp, and fish flesh is flaky. Flakiness can be tested by inserting fork tine into flesh. If flesh flakes freely, fish is finally fried. Once again, work pancake turner between skillet and fish. Remove from skillet and place dramatically on serving platter or directly on dinner plate. Garnish with salt, pepper, and lemon juice as desired.

Step Eight: Devour!

It is important to ignore one's uneasiness at eating food that is staring back. Follow instructions in *How to Bone a Fish* and the dining experience will be delicious. Some seemingly unattractive things provide great satisfaction and joy, such as an exercise and diet program that affords a svelte figure, or the offensive process of hollowing out a pumpkin for Jack O' Lantern carving. Just as one must endure inconvenience to achieve any goal, a fish must look and taste like fish to grant the true feeling of feeding on fish.

How to Bone a Fish

Owing to the frugal nature of the fisherman, it is pertinent that all fish consumers (or those who eat small fried trout) know the proper technique to bone and then partake of fried fish. This should be done out of respect for the time and talents devoted to obtaining a fish for consumption.

It is important to note that the fish fryer (not to be confused with Fish Friar, a religious figure in the fish community) must maintain all head and tail parts attached to said fish.

When presented with a freshly pan fried fish (preferably, trout), the fish consumer must immediately take stock of and assess the difficulty and delicacy of the task at hand. How much talent will it require to remove the crisp skin and tender flesh of said fish without removing the head and tail from the remaining skeletal bones? In other words, how might one eat a fish as does a cartoon cat?

Step One: Begin

Grasp fish by tail fins with left hand. Holding dinner fork in right hand, gently insert one tine under skin at base of tail fin from underside of fish through to center back. This is similar to steering a needle through one layer of fabric rather than jabbing it through the entire garment. Do not catch bones with tine. Gently, but firmly, release skin from tail fins.

Step Two: Removal of Flesh

Continue to hold fish by tail fin. With all four fork tines, gently begin pulling flesh and skin away from fish bones, working in a tail-to-head and back-to-belly motion. The skin along center back may need a little coaxing. If necessary, insert one tine along the center back as described in Step One. Continue until flesh is separated as far as the fish head.

Step Three: Separation of Flesh from Head

Upon arrival at fish head, one fork tine is again inserted under skin at base of head, or where the neck would be if the fish had a neck. Gently tear the skin and drop flesh on plate.

Step Four: To Eat or Not to Eat

A true connoisseur would at this point repeat the first three steps on opposite side of fish body. However, a true fish lover may be inclined to give in to his cravings and dig right in. Whatever the verdict, the remaining flesh needs to be removed from opposite side of fish. This is done by repeating Steps One through Three.

Step Five: Presentation

It is important to properly display boney remains both for reverence to the fallen fish, and as an exhibition of one's talents. Place the skeleton (head and tail intact) across the top of dinner plate being careful to allow just the tip of mouth and the ends of tail fins to artistically extend over edges of dinner plate.

Step Six: Evaluate Efficiency

Prior to consuming tender flesh of fish, it is pertinent to evaluate the thoroughness of removal to determine whether any bones escaped the removal process and remain in the flesh waiting to be consumed and stuck in one's craw. If so, remove them. This is simply ritualistic for the true connoisseur. Failure to complete the task can be hazardous to the true fish lover's general health.

Step Seven: Devour Delicacy

Having properly completed removal, display, and evaluation steps, one may now partake of the tender flesh of fish. This may be done as quickly or as lingeringly as desired. Fish may be garnished with salt, pepper, and lemon juice if the connoisseur/fish lover so chooses. Ingestion of remaining skin is optional.

Hint: Patience is the key. No exercise in frugality was ever achieved in the absence of patience!

If You Can Find It, You Can Eat It

One can grow, capture, or scavenge nearly all the food necessary to survive provided he is patient, strong, and adventurous. Growing up on the family farm, relaxing by a stream, and scouring the mountainside not only provide nourishment to body and soul, these activities also lend a fair amount of practical knowledge and little used tidbits of information.

Grow it. The operative word here is *if.* I recall rows and rows of lush green vegetables in my parent's garden—beets and radishes, beans and corn, squash and tomatoes, cucumbers, carrots, peas, and lettuce. My garden has a couple of scrawny tomato plants and some sick-looking potatoes.

What I don't recall is the transition from planting to harvest. I remember the planting. It required a hoe, some vegetable seeds, two links from a potato harvester, and some bailing twine. The harvester links were driven into the ground at either end of the garden row and bailing twine strung between them. The hoe was used to create a furrow along the twine thus yielding a straight row. Seeds were then dropped at appropriate distances into the furrow, and covered over with a light tap of the foot.

I remember the harvest. My legs ached from squatting to pick beans from the bushes. My stomach hurt from eating too many raw peas. If the ground was too dry, beet, carrot, and radish stems would break off at ground level, requiring a shovel to complete the harvest. Squash don't bounce. Tomatoes have to be covered so they don't freeze before they are ripe. Then they have to be bottled.

I don't remember weeding, watering, and waiting for the vegetables to mature.

My recollection of the harvesting of the farm animals is less pleasant than the harvesting of vegetables.

Chickens really do flop and squawk after their throats have been slit. They smell terrible when dipped in a bucket of hot water to facilitate easy feather removal. The young ones are tender and juicy. The old ones must be stewed for they are as tough as they were ornery while living. If butchering occurs during winter, pink snow also happens.

Ducks make messes everywhere. Their dipped feathers smell worse than the chickens.' Pigs are great for disposing of kitchen waste. Calves grow into stubborn steers. The first two weeks cows are put to pasture their raw milk tastes like the barn.

Capture it. Nothing tastes as good as a rainbow trout caught in Teton Basin. Pheasant is prettier than it tastes. Halibut can be baked, boiled, barbequed, burnt, and brought from Alaska. Venison is more attractive on the hoof than on the plate. Alligator and frog legs really do taste like chicken. Crappie (These are fish—pronounced craw-pea) and perch are only for the very hungry. For the rest of us, they are a waste of time!

Scavenge it. Chicken eggs are the easiest and most useful items to scavenge. Duck eggs are very large and have a strong flavor. Lambsquarter tastes just like spinach and can be harvested from the dirt lane leading to the barn. Beet greens also taste like spinach, but watch out for the bugs! A watercress sandwich with butter and salt is a peppery treat full of Vitamin E. Asparagus and gooseberries demand an acquired taste. Puffball mushrooms really are edible, but only if eaten before they are ripe and foul! Homemade chokecherry syrup beats any other pancake topping, anywhere. Huckleberries pack the most punch; however, they are difficult to find, owing to their popularity with other scavengers—and bears.

Practical knowledge gained from growing, capturing, and scavenging includes: patience, procedure, and purpose. Rushing the growth process will only result in inferior or unripe product. Fishing and hunting require specific techniques for success. Scavenging can be time consuming, but results in the consumption of many exotic and tasty vittles.

Tidbits of little used information are a byproduct of the survival quest that lends satisfaction to those who take pride experiencing life as others may not. Only a true scavenger can say, "I lived off the land, and I *liked* it!"

Can A Cookie Cure A Cold?

In this day of natural health, homeopathic healing, and low-fat everything, it is refreshing to note that a good old chocolate chip cookie is not only a very effective, but often, immediate cure for many ailments. You disagree?

My three-year-old son skinned his knee. He came wailing to find me. Naturally, I was in the kitchen. Tears pouring from his eyes he cried, "I need a cookie!" I leapt to the refrigerator, jerked a zipper bag from the icebox, and produced the miraculous item. He took one bite and promptly announced, "I'm all better now." Amazing, the healing power of the cookie! Not convinced?

My husband of twenty years prefers cookies and milk for breakfast. I've tried to convert him to cold cereal. It has more *natural* and *low-fat* attributes. He tried some brand of wheat flakes for a few days. We couldn't stand him! He was a grouch. So I baked and life was better.

While expecting our last child I was counseled to watch my carbohydrate intake. This was traumatic. "Doctor," I complained, "if I don't have cookies in the house, my family is emotionally unstable!" While one might discount the power of the chocolate chip cookie to heal open wounds, there is no denying its effect on our mental health.

"Pshaw," you say? Consider: Offering of food shows love. We give gifts of food to those we love at Valentines Day, Thanksgiving, and Christmas. If someone gets married, we feed everyone. If a young man wishes to propose or even seduce, he offers chocolates to sweeten his beloved. We show love to newborns by offering mother's milk. We feed our cats.

Offering service shows love. It is an act of service to prepare a meal or a chocolate chip cookie. We work to make a living to buy food to prepare for those we love. Then we prepare it. Then we share it. Then we clean the kitchen! It is true that the simple and few complex carbohydrates in a chocolate chip cookie have a physical effect that produces a quick sense of comfort and well-being. They raise blood sugar levels and taste delicious! But the emotional effect is far greater. A chocolate chip cookie says, "Someone loves me. Someone took an hour and baked this cookie just for me. Someone cares enough about me to know how much I love chocolate!" And love makes all things a little better. Can a cookie cure a cold? Probably not. But hey, it's worth a shot!

Just Because You Can, Doesn't Mean You Should

I married a dairy farmer and soon learned that one of my major responsibilities as a farm wife would be to can and preserve fruits and vegetables for the coming winter. Having avoided these activities for my first twenty-five years, I was apprehensive of the tasks at hand. To my surprise, my initial experience proved a joy rather than a chore!

As our strawberry patch began to show signs of a harvest, my husband of just six months had a hint he was fond of using. "Soon, you'll be able to make strawberry jam!" When the day arrived, I rolled up my sleeves, gritted my teeth, and plunged into my duty. As I stood stirring the thickening jam, I remembered Grandma Nelson—or rather, Grandma Nelson's *Back Porch*. There was an old manual washing machine in the room we referred to as the *Back Porch*. Grandma had been afflicted with a stroke and her ten children shared the burden of caring for her in her own home. I can remember my mother washing clothes in that old machine when we stayed with Grandma after her stroke. My favorite part of Grandma's *Back Porch* was an upright freezer. On the racks inside its door were bottles of strawberry jam. I can't recall what other treats it contained; probably a trout or two from Teton Creek and some frozen corn. I remember opening the freezer door and touching the jars with my fingertips. I would hold my fingers against the glass until the frost melted and tiny windows revealed the red goodies within. Mom would catch me and growl at me for keeping the freezer door open, just as I now growl at my children for similar offenses!

I make strawberry jam every year. Whether I have five jars in my freezer or twenty-five, I complete the ritual. It has become a tradition for me. In a way, it helps to preserve my memory of Grandma, and of Grandma's house, for each time I stir my strawberry jam I recall the first time I made it and the memories come flooding back. I will always keep frosty jars of strawberry jam in my upright freezer just as there were always frosty jars in Grandma Nelson's freezer.

Not every canning project is as rewarding or goes as smoothly as did my strawberry jam efforts. Over the years, countless bottles have refused to seal, bushels of fruit have spoiled before the task was completed, and dozens of filled jars remain on my shelves because the family just doesn't like canned peaches and pears anymore. They never did develop an appetite for the carrots and new potatoes I bottled just because I could. There are those items that remain unidentified because, as a beginner, I wasn't wise enough to label and date the lids. They will never be eaten, but I am reluctant to dispose of them as I am confident they took much effort and time that I didn't have to spare.

Red onions are abundant, free, and pretty. I thought it a good idea to save some for a rainy day. Having located a recipe for Vinegared Red Onions, I filled three dozen pint jars. I have only opened one. The pink onions were nasty! They lost a little color as they were processed, but the onion and vinegar flavors became stronger, too strong to use as a garnish, condiment, or main dish! They aren't even worth using as a decoration, as the color has continued to fade to a dull brown.

I have streamlined my canning and preserving efforts over the years. I now strive to devote my time, talents, and cash to things that will be of use such as green beans, pickled beets, apple pie filling, and frozen corn. Oh, and strawberry jam, because not only is it of sentimental value, it has become a staple in our diet. My family might perish without a freezer full of strawberry jam!

When All Else Fails, Bake

Baking is a survival skill believed to have been handed down for generations. What supports this theory? A long line of incredibly good cooks with robust husbands! What validates a woman's existence more than laying food before her family? Not just any food, mind you, but food prepared by her own hands, in her own kitchen in the home she shares with those she loves. Her mission is to nurture. Her aim is to please. Okay, enough for corny. Here's how one goes about using cooking as a survival skill.

The door bell rang this morning and I rushed to see who it might be, hoping it wasn't a salesman or worse, a missionary of another faith! To my surprise there stood a friend bearing gifts—five very large, very fresh, very sweet, cinnamon rolls! They were a "thank you" for participating in a program that I had murmured about for several days. Although I felt a twinge of guilt over my reluctance to perform, I was ever so pleased with the offering. I thanked her profusely, offered my assistance if she ever needed it in the future, resolved not to partake of an entire roll all in one sitting, shut the door, and devoured my first roll! My memory of the dreaded program grew fonder. My friend had succeeded in winning me over once again.

What is the power baked goods have over the human race? Consider the time and effort involved in producing such items. Let's start at the very beginning ... planting season. Or maybe that would be the harvest the year before the planting season—or the planting season before that. Hmm. Let's skip planting, harvest, milling, and marketing, and go straight to the kitchen.

Some degree of planning must occur for the cook to produce her goods as desired. If they are to be offered warm and fresh as in cookies, breads, and cinnamon rolls, timing is crucial. If they are to be offered cooled and aged as jelly rolls or cheesecakes, a greater allowance of time is important. Baked goods are not a last minute afterthought. In the case of my Aunt Ella, they were a true labor of love. Aunt Ella used an old cook stove until 1975. Yes, the kind one built a fire inside for heat. *Ella's Bread* was always warm and fresh, and it was ever available. *Ella's Bread* was some of the best bread around, and she produced it by first learning to keep her cook stove stoked and the temperature just right. My family thinks I'm spoiling them when I make dough in my bread machine, roll it out, and bake it in my electric oven!

There is a physical effort required to produce a baked treat. Whether stoking, kneading and rolling, or simply measuring ingredients and flipping a switch, one must *do* something to bring forth the tasty product. This simple act can cure a myriad of ailments and I am assured, it will keep the devil away! For instance, boredom can quickly be cured with a recipe book and a few items from the pantry. Not that most folks have an opportunity to experience boredom. In fact, I would suggest the same cure for hunger, aggravation, depression, or that other affliction one often experiences—"I have too many things to do and not enough time in which to do them!" Fix a treat. The family won't care what else you have accomplished all day.

Baked goods serve as a solution to various other difficulties ranging from a tight budget to the need for an appropriate gift. Flour will always be cheaper than beef. Biscuits or rolls will stretch the use of beef, or chicken, or fish. A teenage boy will require less protein for dinner if he has snatched three or four hot rolls before the meal begins! Bread and butter can make even clear broth appear satisfying. Another budget stretcher? If the house is chilly, bake something. It will warm the kitchen and fill up that teenage boy, thus killing two birds with one roll! Need to instill a desire to follow instructions? What better object lesson than a cake minus the baking soda, or cookies minus the sugar? Do you feel fat? Bake something then contemplate how hard you're going to diet and workout while eating the freshly baked goodie. When afflicted with an identity crisis, it is valuable to cook something and then offer it to those you love. You will discover, once again, that you are a nourisher, a provider, a lover. Baked goods are always appropriate gifts for new neighbors, new mothers, classroom teachers, and those in mourning. It's difficult to go wrong when offering food. Need to impress someone? Put a pile of frosting on top of something from your oven.

Working in one's kitchen can rejuvenate. It can provide an opportunity for education, meditation, and mystification. Rejuvenation occurs from identifying with one's purpose and refueling one's body and soul. Even trying a new recipe can provide renewed interest in a tedious task and offer an opportunity to learn a new technique or skill. Meditation. Those people that live in your house will get out of your way if they think leaving you alone will speed the treat making process. Use this time to create a tried and true recipe that requires little focus, thus permitting one to dwell on important issues such as, "What will I fix for dinner tomorrow?" It will also offer a chance to connect with the past. Taste and smell are vivid memory triggers. My mother's big green bowl—I believe it was Tupperware, predecessor to the big yellow bowl, the big orange bowl, and the current big white bowl with handle—was the first container in which I remember yeast activating. It often contained very large batches of pumpkin cookie dough. Her aluminum turkey roaster was actually a mixing bowl for popcorn balls and stuffing. Mystification. Who hasn't had an *experience* in the kitchen? Once, a ghost appeared. It was actually the baby of the family clothed in diaper and flour bin contents. Unleavened bread happens—by accident. Sometimes the leavening is just slow as in the case of the mushrooming field batch, a result of Aunt Mary's uncertainty and attempt to hide the evidence. What about the Miner accusing Esther of baking cookies for him when he knew for certain they were actually biscuits?

Procrastination is one of the greatest reasons for baking. Who can question one's purpose while in the kitchen? Remember, thou art the provider of the food, the nurturer of the family, the cook. I will choose baking over any other domestic task, especially toilet cleaning and lawn mowing. I will put off making a necessary phone call because it might distract me from the oven timer. I want to write a book, but I'm afraid of failure so I will cook something instead. It will put off rejection for awhile! Besides, baking is important. It requires action and Proverbs 19:15 states "idle souls shall suffer hunger." When all else fails, bake!

CHAPTER THREE

Felines and Feathers

I Wish I Were a Cat

Everybody needs a family cat. Although the Miner claimed he hated cats, they were ever present. In town, out of town, on a ranch or at a mine, cats were somewhere about. We always had one, or twelve. That's the thing about cats, they are ever available. They are adaptable. They can take you or leave you. A cat can be needy, or not. A cat will nap without guilt. A cat never has to fix her hair. A cat will love unconditionally.

Cats reproduce like rabbits! Not that I would ever want to be so prolific, but consider the overall experience the mother cat enjoys. Gestation lasts only a few weeks, unlike the eternity it takes human mothers to produce their young. Labor normally occurs overnight with little to no disturbance of her owner's rest. She lactates easily and receives a massage in the process. When she is bored with her feeding young, she stands up and walks away. Her girlish figure returns almost immediately, as does her ability to engage in reproductive activity! She cares not whether her neighbor cat had three kittens or six, nor how quickly her neighbor cat resumed mouse hunting. She just does the job. She bears her young, feeds them, teaches them to hunt, and sends her adolescents into the world to fend for themselves. Then she does it again!

Cats are not particular about their accommodations, at least, not until they have claimed possession. They can live in or out of doors, depending on the need of their owner and the nature of their surroundings. Cats can make a home of a haystack, a car engine, a cardboard box, or an empty easy chair. They do, however, become very possessive of their territory once they have developed a routine! Cats often prefer high places from which to view the world. Whether this is simply for a better vantage point during a hunt, or to establish his superiority to the rest of the world, is not known. Superiority is the most probable answer.

Felines are creatures of habit. Once established, his routine will vary little from day to day. Unlike the restless human, he is okay with this. The current family cat has created his own path in the grass around flowerbeds and trees. He enters the front door to exit through the back, waiting patiently, sometimes annoyingly, for an opening when he could easily arrive in the back yard of his own accord in a much more timely fashion. He knows when to come in at night, and when the household should be stirring each morning. He is oblivious to daylight savings time!

A cat is self-reliant. She doesn't really need an owner, but enjoys the convenience of being fed. However, she will continue to hunt, as her inner lioness urges. Few preparations need be made to leave a cat alone. Unless she has been conditioned to rely on others, she can find food and water as needed. She will often find food when not needed, thus presenting it to her owner as a gift on a step just outside the door. Oh, to cook simply for the joy of it! Her fur coat is fashionable and functional no matter the weather. She is satisfied with her attire and takes time, as needed to groom self and others.

Cats are indulgent—without guilt! They will sleep entire days away giving one the old *squint eye* if disturbed before the nap is finished. Their grooming routine is lengthy, often followed by another nap. They prefer the human lap, when available, for reclining purposes, expressing their satisfaction and comfort with loud rumbling purrs. They are quick to let one know if she has inconvenienced her feline friend. They know what they want, they take it, and they have no difficulty expressing their needs and opinions.

Cats are fierce.

Chiropractors are nonexistent in the world of cats. If only my back would bend like that! Even the smallest kitten quickly learns to take a moment to realign before taking on the world. The process appears enjoyable and ritualistic, aiding in his confidence and ability to face the challenges that loom ahead. One could learn a lot from a cat.

I wish I were a cat. If only I could avoid cleaning myself with my tongue and eating raw mice!

And Then There Are Black Cats

I have known cats; yellow cats, grey cats, calico cats, and Siamese; but the most catlike of cats have always been black. Maybe it is the likeness to their larger cousins, the panther or puma, but black cats seem to epitomize feline character. Consider some cat qualities that are better suited to those of the black coat.

Stealth. Cats are nocturnal predators. They stalk their prey at night. A black cat has so much the advantage as he is hidden by the dark, his glowing eyes the only warning sign.

Vanity. Spending hours on his grooming routine, his dark coat outshines his more colorful peers.

Bloodline. Unlike those with markings indicating a mixed breed, he is black. His lineage may be contaminated, but his appearance will not betray him.

I have known two noteworthy black cats. One female. One male. Their stories follow.

Licorice, obviously named for her coloring, was a prolific female bearing two litters per summer. I acquired her when I was an apartment dweller. She was an inside/out cat, taking her food and rest indoors and her adventures out of doors. Thus, the proliferation! My roommate who was also my sister, had acquired a pet as well—Cletus, a yellow canary. I have never been fond of pets that could not contribute to the common welfare by killing mice or licking wounds. Cletus could do neither. I was somewhat distressed, however, when I returned home one day to find Licorice with a single yellow feather clinging to her chin and no other sign of Cletus! It was this incident, and the second batch of kittens, that precipitated Licorice's relocation to the family farm. Licorice adapted to farm life quite nicely continuing to produce twelve to sixteen kittens every summer.

Cats have a higher level of intelligence than do dogs. Live with it Dog Lovers! While a cat will stalk her prey, patiently waiting for opportune moments to attack, a dog will bound headlong into his target without pause for strategy or caution. So it happened that Licorice wreaked havoc on another of my siblings' pets. Ted's bird dog, Cindy (Why don't Dog Lovers name their pets with a little more dignity?), having spent many years living off her keepers, was getting on in age and had taken to accompanying the family on most trips. They happened to be visiting the farm while Licorice was rearing a young batch of kittens. She had secured them in a small hot house Esther had constructed near the back door. Esther was rearing chicks, ducks, geese, and peacocks. An electric fence had been erected to corral the peacocks. While the visitors were enjoying the summer weather, Esther warned Ted, "Better not let

Cindy go into the hot house. Licorice has her kittens in there!" His answer, "Oh, you're not afraid of a little old house cat, are you Cindy?" Cindy (not as smart as a cat) determined to display her bravery by immediately entering the hot house and exiting even more rapidly amongst a commotion of yips and yelps. She bounded headlong into a parked car! In very dog-like fashion, she picked herself up and continued yipping and bounding until she made contact with the electric fence! It is a wonder she didn't give up the ghost then and there. Sometime later, she recovered and avoided the hot house that was home to the miniature black panther and cubs for the remainder of the visit.

Are cats people, too? Roger (now see if you can follow this) named after the original owner of his predecessor, Panther, who was also black and had been unfortunately flattened like a pancake, developed many habits and traits similar to those of the *Homo sapiens*. Let us examine.

Roger likes his morning routine. As owners, we created that routine by offering him a small bit of milk in an empty jar lid. Now, just as so many cannot begin their day without a fresh cup of caffeine, Roger enters the house, waits for his bit of milk, and then exits the house to make his morning rounds.

Roger owns the garage. His food and water are there and he allows us to park a vehicle in his domain. He often knocks, yes knocks, on the door to indicate his desire to enter. Have I seen this? No. However, there is no mistaking the rapping sound, or the black cat entering the room when the door is opened. Others only believe it when they are fortunate enough to personally witness the knocking. He prefers the doorbell for the exterior doors! Believe it or not!

Roger offers gifts. On occasion, when he is feeling generous, he will bring his "catch of the day," a small bird or mouse, and present it as an offering on the step outside the door. I can never bring myself to consume such delectable treats! Smart though, attempting bribery like that.

Every cat is black when I read fiction. (My apologies Ms. Braun) Halloween cats are black. What self respecting witch would own a yellow tabby? It must have been black cats that inspired the phrase, "cats have nine lives." If you've seen one black cat ... no, if you've seen several black cats, you may think you've seen one. Poor silly dog Cindy, she saw one black cat. It almost ended her life!

How to Slay a Rooster

Roosters are larger and more combative than the usual frying chicken. On occasion it becomes necessary to remove a rooster from the barnyard community. This is most commonly accomplished by slaying him. The rooster's combative nature is often the catalyst to his demise. Rooster slaying differs from chicken butchering as it requires greater strength and determination.

Step One: Get Attacked by Rooster

Due to their combative nature, roosters are prone to defend the barnyard when necessary and when unnecessary. Many a red rooster has jumped upon an unsuspecting shoulder, given a quick peck of the flesh, and shortly landed in a stewing pot. So it was for Captain Bonneville. He hopped upon Esther's shoulder and drew blood from her neck one too many times.

Step Two: Get Mad

Get really, really mad! Repeated rooster attacks can become annoying to the point of enragement. This will cause an instant surge of adrenaline. The adrenaline rush associated with rooster attacks and neck bleeding will afford one the added determination necessary for rooster slaying.

Step Three: Locate Weapon

Having become extremely irate and spirited, it will not be difficult to march swiftly to the house and obtain large butcher knife. Although it is sometimes difficult to remember where exactly items have been stored, the location of butchering weapon will be extremely clear to the offended chicken owner.

Step Four: Enlist Help

Although one is aided by ire and adrenaline, roosters can still be difficult to catch. It may be wise to enlist the assistance of family members. This should not be difficult as they will quickly respond after observing one's torn and bleeding neck. Be certain all parties protect neck and shoulders as the combative rooster may be inclined to attack again.

Step Five: Catch Rooster

When the rooster has been cornered, grab both of his feet and tuck his head under one wing. This will prevent him from pecking, after all, that particular infraction is the reason he is about to die!

Step Six: Locate Butchering Surface

Find a big rock, tree stump, or fence post. Do not use a rock that is engraved and used as a decorative lawn ornament. Its appeal may be lessened by the following process. It is best to carry out the deed away from high traffic areas, especially those frequented by vegans and publicists!

Step Seven: Hesitate

The red rooster has been a part of the barnyard community for some time. He was a cute chick before he grew into a combative rooster. One may take a moment to ensure ire is sufficient for rooster slaying. Observe blood on collar and shirtsleeve. This should be enough motivation to proceed.

Step Eight: Continue

Still holding rooster by both legs, place his head and neck on butchering surface. While positioning butcher knife above head in preparation for delivering fatal blow, avoid getting pecked yet again. Red roosters are not only combative, they are tenacious as well. Deliver blow. This is sometimes called *wringing his neck*, a reference to more primitive butchering techniques.

Step Nine: Cleanup

After having had his neck wrung, red rooster will continue to aggravate as he hops and flops leaving a trail of red residue. He may soil ones attire still more. A garden hose will prove handy in washing away the red residue. Once he has given up the fight, it will be necessary to de-feather him and prepare him for stewing. This process is smelly and tedious, and may need to be discussed at a later date.

Although the butchering and cleanup process is unpleasant and can become lengthy, ridding the barnyard of said red rooster is a positive move. In his misguided efforts to protect, the red rooster created a negative environment. One may now enter the area safely to feed remaining chickens, collect eggs, and see to the overall welfare of the barnyard community.

Obstacles often present themselves in life—fear, lack of confidence, fatigue, or sin. The process required to overcome those obstacles may be unpleasant and sometimes lengthy, but it will most often prove positive. Surmounting the obstacle will allow one to go forward, to continue on the path, to reap the rewards of determination, at least until another red rooster raises his ugly beak!

Egg Gathering and Chick Hatching

Esther was an egg gatherer and a chicken raiser. Her six daughters claim she also raised some great looking chicks! It is, however, the barnyard variety that will be discussed here. As poultry has become increasingly popular in the modern diet it is important to understand its origins.

Laying hens are amazingly tolerant of the intruding gatherer reaching under their warm under parts to discover a freshly laid egg. Sometimes one will utter a cluck or ruffle a wing, but often the laying hen will complain very little over the disturbance. She knows her duty. Her calling in life is to provide the versatile protein source that most cooks cannot do without. She will regularly drop an egg for her mistress, so long as her needs are met. Her needs are simple—shelter, water, and food. No, she needn't have a rooster in the barnyard. He is only required by the setting hens. This is fortunate as the farm wife is likely to have carried out the instructions in the previous chapter. The laying hen will, however, cease to lay eggs if deprived of feed. The barnyard hen can often scavenge her own food. Summertime she will forage on weeds, small bugs, and vegetable gardens if the garden is not sufficiently protected. Her eggs will sport a fine golden yolk, nearly orange, resulting from the organic freshness of her feed. She may even show off on occasion and produce a double yolk egg.

A coop hen needs a little more attention as she is confined. So long as she receives her feed, she too will regularly provide the desired product. However, her yolks will be a lighter more anemic looking yellow due to the lack of fresh greens and insects in her diet. If her caregivers neglect to provide the proper nourishment, she will discontinue egg laying as she will be using her reserves to stay alive!

It is important for the novice egg gatherer to understand the delicate procedure of procuring eggs. Although, the egg exits the hen's body much as any other matter, an experienced egg layer is particular about the conditions of her laying area. Her nest will be neat and clean as she takes pride in her life's work. One must approach her with confidence and calm. Look her in the eye—not the opposite end! Gently slide one's hand beneath her under side. Her belly feathers will be soft and warm. Continue reaching until egg is located or until it becomes apparent she has not yet provided one. Take hold of egg and just as gently, retrieve egg and/or hand from beneath the hen. She may take notice, she may not.

If the barnyard is equipped with a rooster, the laying hen may convert to setting hen. Not to worry. One of two directions may be taken. Although there is a rooster in the yard, eggs are still edible, provided they are gathered daily and kept cool. Even though a hen may be *setty* (The act of staying on her nest to warm eggs and thus provide chicks), she may continue to service as a laying hen so long as her eggs are removed from her nest each day. She will require feed and water delivered as she will stubbornly remain on her nest most of the time.

If the setting hen is allowed to retain eggs in her nest, she will keep them warm and rotated for about twenty-one days. This will produce happy healthy chicks. She will vacate her nest for a few minutes each day to tend to her private needs. If one is fortunate to discover her absence, he may take the opportunity to view the progress of the maturing eggs. This will prove a waste of one's time as an egg containing a yolk looks exactly as an egg with a chick growing inside. Only when chicks are full term and beginning their outbreak may one hear soft peeping sounds and pecking noises. Small cracks may be visible as shell begins to give way. Do not *help* in removal of shell! Chick must complete this task on his own.

Upon examination of nest, one may become alarmed as broken shells will be apparent, but chicks may not. Do not immediately blame the neighborhood weasel. Chicks are likely hiding in their mother's wings. This is done to provide warmth and protection. A hen can hide ten chicks in her wing feathers much more easily than the human mother can hide ten pounds in her jeans! Upon further examination one will likely discover several small chicks peeking from the wings and back feathers of their mother.

It is possible, even easy to *graft* chicks to a setting hen. This is done most often by stealing eggs from a fertile laying hen (remember the rooster must be present) and placing them in the nest of the setting hen. She will accept them as her own, keep them warm and rotated, and mother them as her own once they have hatched. Not only will she adopt another hen's eggs, but she will often accept the eggs of ducks and other fowl just as readily. Ducklings, being larger in body than chicks, have more difficulty hiding amongst her wing feathers.

It is also possible to hatch chicks in the absence of a setting hen. One must first gather eggs from a hen that has been keeping company with a rooster. The eggs must then be incubated and rotated for success. Incubators are a simple warming device equipped with a light for heat and a fan for circulation. First, check with a local farm store to determine proper temperature. Second, be sure to rotate eggs daily. It is a mystery of nature that a hen can rotate each of her eggs at precisely the correct time and angle to allow for healthy happy chicks. Incubated chicks are not always so fortunate. Man can set a clock, count eggs, mark them with a pencil to track rotation, keep accurate records, maintain constant temperature, and still produce a brood presenting twenty-five percent with birth defects! Defects range from undersized wings, to misshapen legs or backwards feet, to blindness. How can a hen do a better job than man?

It is important in life to understand one's role. What is the most valuable use of one's time? Where should he focus his efforts? One could learn much from a chicken. A laying hen knows her role. Her responsibility is to eat and produce one egg everyday. She does so and gladly gives up her egg as she will need the nest space for the morrow. A setting hen knows her role. Her duty is to the unborn and the very young. She must keep them protected and prepared for the future. When they can forage on their own she grants them independence. The rooster knows that his job is to be brightly colored, loud, arrogant, and to protect and serve as many hens as he can locate. He must also avoid the butcher knife of an irate farm wife!

Whether one's responsibility is to provide, nurture, or protect, he will find the most fulfillment in completing his duties regularly and accurately. If he has the pleasure of looking good, as does the rooster, while carrying out those obligations, his joy and satisfaction will be complete!

Electric Fences

Some barriers were never meant to be broken. Take, for instance, the electric fence. Its purpose, as with any fence, is either to keep something in or to keep something out. To the resourceful Miner, a length of wire and a source of electricity could serve a myriad of purposes. They also produced a fair amount of hazards.

When one is attempting to live off the land, it is pertinent that he strive to protect that which he is living off of. Cattle can be confined to a pasture with the aid of a simple electric fence. Here they can graze as needed and remain safe from traffic of passing automobiles. The expense of constructing such a barrier is minimal. Low risk—high return. A quick zap of electricity, though viewed as cruel and unusual by some city folks, is short lived and harmless. If there is any doubt, just ask a farm kid. He has surely experienced the jolt and lived to tell about it!

While poultry is an economical and relatively simple product to raise, chickens, ducks, geese, and turkeys can and will wreak havoc on a country garden. Therefore, it is important to protect the garden from winged intruders. This can be done in a variety of ways. Plastic snakes can be hung around the garden to scare off fowl. This method is highly ineffective. Chicken wire can be erected as a fence to keep them out, but it is cumbersome and more expensive than plastic snakes. It is better suited for use as a sweet pea trellis, parade float framework, or in fabrication of rabbit pens. Scarecrows are for looks. Enter the *hot fence*.

Simple in construction and design, an electric fence can be erected in almost any necessary location. One is merely restricted by the length of wire available and location of the electricity source. On occasion, it is necessary to become creative with the actual building of the *hot fence*. Enter the Miner.

One of the Miner's well rehearsed lines was, "If a person had" ... followed by some item such as "a board about so long ... a couple of screws about this big ... or, enough wire." These words always preceded a project, even an invention at times that often resulted in the simplification of a task, the solving of a problem, or the creation of a new game or form of entertainment. The electric fence served all of these purposes.

Having strung a length of wire from the electricity source in the barn, over the parking area, attaching it to a post, and descending it to garden level, the Miner was able to surround his vegetable production area with a simple barrier that could be turned on and off with the flip of a switch, thus protecting the patch from would be scavengers. Problem solved. Enter the Entertainment.

It has not been determined whether elephants never forget, or if elephants never remember—probably, the latter. So it is with farm fowl, hunting dogs, and Miners. One would expect that chickens, ducks, and turkeys, might have trouble recalling where it was that they felt that last tingling jolt and repeatedly encounter the hot fence. They are, after all, mostly occupied with egg laying, rooster avoiding, and bug and plant eating. When a chicken comes into contact with an electric wire, and she will as she is determined to partake of the garden's gifts, there is an immediate clamor of squawking and feather flapping as the offended fowl issues her complaint to the rest of the barnyard and world. One might expect her eggs to arrive hard boiled! Her brief memory will allow her to repeat the experience time and again.

Hunting dogs, on the other hand, ought to be brighter than the species they were bred to hunt! One might suppose that given the opportunity to observe birds colliding with hot fences, a hunting dog would be prudent enough to give the fence a wide berth. The problem with hunting dogs is they have one track minds. "Catch something and bring it back. Catch something and bring it back. Catch something and bring it back!" Whether a black cat, a Frisbee, or a bird colliding with an electric wire, a hunting dog will bound toward his prey oblivious of the hazards and *hot fences* along the way. If a chicken can create a squawking feathery ruckus, a bird dog can create a yipping, howling blur that eventually hides in a corner licking its wounds until the next tantalizing prey wanders near, yes, the electric fence!

An electric fence is not a large physical barrier obviously in the way and difficult to see beyond. It is unique in that it can be turned *On* and *Off*, thus becoming weak and ineffective when not in use. It can become almost nonexistent. The trouble is, those who build *hot fences* often forget whether the fence is *Off*, or *On*. There is a very quick way to find out! Prudent as it may be to locate the switch to resolve the question, it is time saving to simply *run into* the fence. Apparently, that was the Miner's preferred mode of determination. Time and again, he would present himself at a gathering with a knot on his head resulting from contact with the wire descending from post to garden level. The contact with the wire did not produce the knot; however, contact with the ground upon reaction from contact with the wire *was* responsible for the knot! Ironically, the Miner was forever warning his guests to be careful of the *hot wire* around the garden. Evidently, he did not want his loved ones experiencing the trauma inflicted upon fowls, hunting dogs, and Miners!

One will encounter barriers in his life. Some are challenges to overcome. Some are bold and apparent. Others are more subtle and require pondering to determine their purpose. There are barriers that exist for the sole purpose of keeping one safe. It is wise to observe others who have attempted to cross those barriers. They will often experience pain, and occasionally, they will refuse to learn, returning to experience still more pain. It is a mistake to believe that the barrier won't hurt, or that this time the electrical source will be turned *Off*. Better to give the barrier a wide berth. If one must know for sure, be patient, someone else is sure to test and discover if the fence is hot!

CHAPTER FOUR

Risky Recreation

So You Want to Buy a Boat

Are you nuts! Maybe you should wreck someone else's boat first. There are a few facts regarding boat ownership that one should be familiar with prior to purchasing a boat of his own. These guidelines may very well save one's sanity.

The first and probably most important guideline is to buy a used boat. Do not be tempted by the shiny paint and bright propeller of a new boat. The unblemished interior and perfect upholstery will not add to the level of fun experienced by boaters. Rather, they will elevate the level of stress the inexperienced boat owner will encounter while developing his boating skills. Look for a well loved boat—one that has previously missed the trailer while loading, scraped up against an unkempt dock, had its propeller dinged by unseen rocks, and/or possesses rebuilt gears having had them stripped by a sandbar. This will not only reduce stress levels, it will also save a great deal of money and grief.

Money. Remember there are hidden costs to boat ownership. Though the monthly payments seem manageable, do not forget the rising costs of insurance, boat fuel, boat licenses, life jackets and boating toys, picnic lunches, boat storage, doctor appointments, insurance deductibles for boat repair, swimsuits, sunglasses, sunscreen, ibuprofen, and a new hot tub.

Grief. A boat can tear a hole in one's heart in so many ways. The first time it gets damaged the owner may feel as if one of his children has been diagnosed with an incurable fungus. This will most likely occur on the maiden voyage in any number of fashions. If one is fortunate enough to have previous trailer experience, the jackknifed boat trailer may be avoided. If not, SUV may experience paint job damage, as well. It is inevitable that the driver of the boat will, at some point, miss the trailer while attempting to load boat. Hailstorms happen. Upholstery wears out. Some reservoirs have hidden obstacles such as, rocks, tree stumps, and sandbars. Boat plugs are small and cheap, but critical to boat buoyancy. Do not forget the plug!

The second guideline is to get help. Boats are not cars. They do not move like cars. They do not steer like cars. They do not have brakes. The steering wheel is on the right side of the boat, not the left. A valid driver's license does not guarantee competent operation of a boat. It is advisable to take a lesson, take a friend (with boating experience), or hire a driver!

Bodies of water can be deceiving. Water, unlike pavement, is fluid. It is ever changing. What may lie well beneath the surface this week may be lurking just below the water line next week, especially if the body of water is an irrigation reservoir during a drought year. It is advisable to take a map, take a friend (that knows the area), or use a depth finder. The latter is probably not the best option as this is a well loved boat. It lost its depth finder long ago.

Weather is unpredictable. Thunder. Lightening. Wind. Rain. Hail. It is advisable to get a weather report, get the boat out of the water, and get to cover.

The third guideline is to exercise patience. Not only is the boat owner new at this activity, the boat riders are also new.

Communication skills tend to develop slowly. While driver can see individual in water behind boat or in front of trailer waiting to help with loading, he cannot hear due to the roar of the motor and propeller. There is a learning curve required to decipher hand signals, head nods, and arm wavings.

Remember, well loved boat was purchased for a reason. It requires practice to learn to enter a boat free of muddy feet. It also requires practice to tie secure knots. Nervous drivers sometimes do bring the propeller into contact with foreign objects. It only takes a few minutes to swamp a boat, but boat will drain and dry provided it can be rescued in time. Keep spare boat plug in glove box.

The fourth guideline is to find joy in the ride. The motivation behind acquiring a boat was most likely to have a good time, spend time with loved ones, and relax. It may take awhile to accomplish this goal. It is difficult to have a good time or relax while panicking over learning to launch, load, and operate one's newly purchased boat. Add a few scrapes and dings, discover that the boat still floats, learn to water ski or catch a fish, improve communication skills, and the experience will begin to be enjoyable. If, however, the motivation was to keep up with the Joneses, the best bet would be to purchase a brand new boat complete with shiny paint job and bright propeller. It would then be wise to park it in a rental storage unit to preserve the newness, take a few snapshots, and talk really big to the neighbors. The monthly payments and insurance will still be due, however many of the added hidden expenses will be avoided—as will the joy.

Moral: If you love something enough, even its imperfections are beautiful.

How to Water Ski

If man were meant to walk on water, he would have been born during the Ice Age. However, there is valor in the attempt. Humility is key—that, and the ability to follow instructions.

Step One: Locate a Boat

It is not necessary to own a boat in order to perfect the skills required for effective water skiing. Accompanying another boat owner is perfectly acceptable. The boat needn't be of competition quality; however, it is pertinent that it can run and is accompanied by an experienced driver.

Step Two: Don a Life Jacket

Second only to the boat, a life jacket is the most important piece of equipment one will employ while learning to water ski. The reason is most obvious; one will spend considerable time in the water.

The life jacket must fit properly, meaning it should very nearly squeeze the air out of one's lungs. This will prevent skier from slipping through the bottom of the life jacket and into the watery depths beneath.

Step Three: Put on Ski Gloves

Gloves provide a look of finesse. They exude skill and confidence. The true purpose for glove wearing while skiing is to enable one to actually hold onto the rope handle long enough to learn the sport.

Step Four: Grab Rope Handle

Step Five: Get in the Water

This step may be accomplished in any number of ways. A woman will usually enter the water in a controlled fashion, climbing onto the swim deck or ladder and easing herself into the lake. A man will make a greater production by jumping from the highest point on the boat, into the air, and coming down in a great splash, soaking everyone in the vicinity.

Step Six: Do not *let go of the rope!*

Step Seven: Put on Water Skis

This step may very well take the most time and patience, both for the skier and for the boat driver. However, careful study of these instructions may lessen the complications. Water skis are buoyant. They sometimes appear to have a mind of their own. The good news is they are ambidextrous. Unless one is attempting to slalom (ski on one ski only), there is no need to be concerned with right or left feet.

Grab the front and back of the boot (it looks like a big shoe) in two hands. If applying the ski to right foot first, the right hand should grab the front of the boot while the left hand grabs the back of the boot. This is important so as not to roll onto one's back while sliding foot into boot. Use opposite hands for opposite foot. Bring knee of said foot into contact with life jacket previously donned. Pull front and back of boot away and diagonal from one another. Wriggle foot into boot. Stop. Take a few resting breaths and try again. Caution: Once ski is applied, resist the urge to roll face forward to rest. This may result in drowning!

Step Eight: Repeat Step Seven—Opposite Foot

Step Nine: Locate Ski Rope

If, while attempting to maneuver feet into ski boots, one has lost grip on rope, it is important to regain possession of said rope. Find the rope. If it is possible to reach the rope—grab it. If it is not possible, the experienced boat driver will then circle around and deliver the rope handle into skier's hands. Remain calm. The driver is better at this than the beginning skier.

Step Ten: Get Into Position

While the driver is delivering the rope, it is wise to take advantage of the opportunity to maneuver the water skis. Remember, skis are buoyant. Having ignored the Caution: in Step Seven, skier will discover that his skis are not only behind his back, but crossed over one another in an inconvenient position. Do not attempt to bring them in front of body by straightening legs and swinging skis forward. This will result in immediate submersion of upper body. One must first roll to his side, then straighten legs and swing skis across the surface of the body of water. When legs are straight, roll onto back and dip rear of skis into the water. Heavy front half of skis will sway back and forth, crossing and uncrossing while skier frantically attempts to force them upright. Ignore skis. Fighting them will result in yet another face first position and require a second attempt at righting oneself.

Skis must be controlled from the hip. Bend knees and adopt a position as if sitting on a chair. Pull feet and skis towards body. This is important! Failure will result in frustration. Maintain chair sitting position.

Place rope and handle between knees. Hold handle firmly in gloved hands while driver begins to bring the rope taut. Rear of boat will promptly appear in view between knees. Maintain chair sitting position.

Step Eleven: Hit It!

When nerves are under control, rope is taut, and boat is in view, yell "Hit it!" Driver will then engage throttle and boat with attached rope and skier will begin to move. Hang on and maintain chair sitting position! Skis will rise out of the water with smiling skier aboard. Enjoy ride until crash.

Step Twelve: Let go of the rope!

Step Thirteen: Recovery

After forgetting to let go of the rope, thus being dragged several yards through the water appearing as a human torpedo, skier will have irrigated sinus cavities and may experience a slight headache. Inventory all body parts. They may be bruised, possibly broken, but should still be attached.

Locate skis. They will be floating somewhere in the lake, probably upside down, and in better shape than the skier.

Locate boat. Experienced driver will be arriving shortly to pick up the pieces. Ski rope should still be connected to boat.

Lie back and relax. A very snug life jacket will keep one afloat until rescuers arrive. Be prepared for great guffaws from experienced skiers. They have all enjoyed the same torture! Admit through chattering teeth that the offer of a wetsuit was actually a good idea, and in the future all pride will be set aside so as to wriggle into the wetsuit for prevention of hypothermia.

Step Fourteen: Climb Back Into the Boat

Having expended much strength and body heat, it is now critical that one muster all courage and pull oneself out of the water and into the boat. The benefits of the buoyant life jacket quickly become a hindrance as it has taken on a great deal of water and weighs approximately one third as much as the skier.

Ski gloves, however, prove valuable once again. They provide the grip one's shaking hands cannot. Set pride aside and allow fellow boaters to grab life jacket and haul one aboard.

Step Fifteen: Elation

Lie on any available flat surface, huffing and puffing, and allow the realization to set in that one has very nearly walked on water. (It's as close as you'll get!) Begin to giggle hysterically while dry towels are offered. Resolve to ski again!

How to Drop a Ski

Having mastered the art of getting out of the water on two skis, making a few snaking turns across the wake, and letting go of the ski rope prior to exhaustion resulting in a crash, the intermediate water skier will inevitably have a desire to advance his skill level. It is now time to attempt to slalom—the art of skiing on one ski. It is best to begin with two skis and purposely lose one of them, all the while remaining above the water, maintaining hold of the ski rope, and moving in a forward direction.

Note: This is an exercise in self control.

Step One: Balance on One Ski

It would be disastrous to lose a ski if one cannot maintain his balance on the other ski. Before assuming he can successfully be pulled around a body of water on one ski, it is a good idea to first practice shifting one's weight from two skis to one.

Find a steady spot in the water in the dark green area to either side of the frothy white water immediately behind the propeller, or in the calmer, undisturbed water just outside the boat's wake. Gently shift one's weight to the dominant leg. (The dominant leg would be that leg with which one is most comfortable holding his weight upon.) Gently! Slowly lift less dominant leg, ever so slightly. Maintain this position for a time until confidence is gained. Slowly shift weight equally to both legs and rest for a moment ... *Do Not* make any swift corrections!

Step Two: Begin Again

Having panicked and over corrected, skier finds himself in a watery mess and must start over. This is a good opportunity to check skis. Slalom ski will have an extra boot. This ski should be placed on dominant leg so as to allow foot of less dominant leg to slide into extra boot behind dominant foot. This is called the toe plate. Muster courage and try again.

Step Three: Repeat Balancing Act

Repeat Step One, this time holding ski of less dominant leg higher out of the water and maintaining balance. Once this has been accomplished skier is ready to attempt to drop extra ski.

Step Four: Drop Ski

Dropping a ski is often referred to as *kicking* a ski. Although the terms are often interchanged, the difference in the literal meaning is significant. *Do Not* literally *kick* the extra ski in an attempt to remove it from the less dominant leg. It is not necessary to use great force to remove the ski, nor is it wise. *Kicking* will result in damage to something. Loss of balance will first occur, attempt will be thwarted, and possible bodily injury may result.

Dropping a ski is, once again, a gentle motion. While maintaining balance on dominant leg, cautiously dip tail of extra ski into water. When resistance is detected, begin to wiggle ankle until ski boot is free. Ski should slide easily away. Do not look back or down to make certain it is gone! Do not attempt to locate it at this time. Skis are buoyant. Driver will retrieve it, eventually.

Step Five: Locate Toe Plate

Still maintaining balance, locate toe plate behind dominant foot. It will be approximately one-half step back along tail of ski. Place foot behind boot and, once again, *gently* slide forward into place. Weight may now be distributed evenly on both legs.

Step Six: Evaluate

One of several things just occurred. Skier *kicked* ski, dropped the wrong ski, had difficulty locating toe plate, stepped too forcefully on slalom ski with free foot, or simply panicked. In any event there was a crash and it will require yet another attempt to accomplish the goal.

Step Seven: Repeat Steps Four and Five

Step Eight: Success

Having gently, cautiously, and patiently repeated Steps Four and Five as necessary, skier may now begin to experience the added control and mobility afforded by maneuvering one ski with the strength and stability of two legs. On a normal day, he would discover that he tired less easily, thus allowing more opportunity for experience and improvement. However, not today! Rest is recommended.

Camping We Will Go

I thought camping was all about fun when I was a child. Wells and Esther provided countless camping expeditions that

I assumed were for recreation. I have since concluded that camping trips were actually all about the fish! Camping kept the fishermen and fisherwomen in close range of the fishing hole. Although I am well experienced in *roughing it,* my perspective of sleeping and eating out of doors has evolved over the years.

The beauty of living (if only for a weekend) next to a fishing hole is the chance one gets to enjoy the sound of a babbling brook at night. The soothing noise gently lulls one to sleep, unlike the babbling children residing in the adjacent tent. Folks go to various lengths to imitate the rhythm of the water; everything from purchasing recorded mood sounds to engineering grand waterfalls in their yards. Somehow, the experience is never the same.

While the babbling brook may be soothing to the ear, it is less than desirable for wading and washing of oneself. Soap doesn't lather and folks don't soak in a mountain stream. It takes only a moment for teeth to begin to chatter and joints to stiffen when taking a dip. The bracing temperature of the water and fresh mountain air do, however, serve as a quick refresher. One's toes never become truly clean. Whether wading barefoot in the muddy bottom or retaining one's sneakers, the toes just get neglected. Sit near the campfire for a few moments and the fact that one is not completely fresh will not be noticed.

Campfires are the original multi-taskers. A campfire provides deodorizer, warmth, trash disposal (paper products only please!), safety from bears, heat source for cooking, and entertainment. One may require the aid of the campfire immediately following his hygiene ritual, not only for body odor camouflage, but also to dry his hair, socks, and sneakers. If necessary, large rocks can be heated near the fire and placed in the bottom of a sleeping bag to replace the electric blanket at home. Be certain these are not too hot! As fires are a strong temptation for young boys, it is necessary to supervise at all times, thus eliminating the chance to experience boredom or relaxation.

Sleeping on the ground. Now *there* is a lesson to be learned. If one neglects to properly inspect and prepare his sleeping space, discomfort will ensue. A true camper knows that a rock in the middle of his space can be quite irritating as can be the open space where a rock once was. He will take great care to examine his sleeping area for obstacles before throwing down a tarp and a sleeping bag. A wise, but less tolerant camper, on the other hand, will quickly erect his cot and air mattress before throwing down *his* sleeping bag! In the event of cold overnight temperatures, an extra blanket, thermal underwear, and a hooded sweatshirt are advisable.

Cooking outside is where the recreation value of the camping experience is weak, at least for the cook. Packing, preparing, and preserving temperature of camp food is a trial. Convincing folks that the black flecks in the eggs are pepper not ashes is also a challenge. Threatening them to eat the burnt food or go without is satisfying. The beauty of cooking over a fire is that ruined food can be dumped out of the pan and quickly cremated. It is a great opportunity to teach children to be less picky about what they consume. Camp food is never perfect, sometimes cold, often burnt, and usually lacking an ingredient that was left in the pantry at home. Cleaning up of camp kitchen and dishwashing is comparable to brook bathing. A little grease is likely to remain on cooking utensils, but will go unnoticed as campfire cooking taints all foods with a hint of smoke. This contributes to the overall experience and has been weakly copied by various bar-b-cue establishments in rural areas.

Accommodations, though exciting to an adventurous youth, are inconvenient. Small children fit nicely on a rock or stump when using it as a chair. Larger folks don't. Unfortunately, small children often park themselves in folding chairs provided for adult use and leave the stumps to their elders. Outdoor restrooms are unpleasant. Pack a shovel. Pack insect repellant. Pack baby wipes. Tow a boat along for water skiing and it will supply recreational pleasure as well as additional packing space!

Weather can be disappointing. One is living *out in it.* Rain, wind, and even sunshine can become tiresome when a house dweller is exposed throughout the day. Pack sunscreen. Pack a rain poncho. Pack it all up and go home!

There are lessons to be learned from the camping experience. Be prepared. Be flexible. Learn to do without. Learn to appreciate the modern conveniences with which you have been blessed. It would be noble to camp simply to learn life lessons. Teaching children to endure adversity is a vital role of a parent. However, camping trips have become all about the waterskiing!

Rock Identification

I am a gold miner's daughter. My upbringing was unique in that I gleaned many skills from the mining experience. For instance, I can pan for gold and actually find it if it is present. Another byproduct of my childhood experience is the ability to identify rocks. I would study for hours Dad's book of "Rocks & Minerals" intrigued by the many varieties, colors, and shapes that lay hidden in the earth. Although I never inherited *Gold Fever* from my father, I still find satisfaction in recognizing a specific gem or *not-so-precious* stone. Even some of the more common rocks have value when one understands their qualities and appreciates their individuality.

Gold is not so different than silver in its properties and usefulness. Both can be molded to cradle other gems, or fashioned into chains and works of art on their own. They are found hidden in the earth. While silver is more useful in industry, gold is valued more for its visual appeal.

Mica can be crushed and added to paints and finishes to provide a metallic appearance. It has little strength of its own, and can be peeled away in layers thin enough one can see right through.

Opals are unique in their depth and color. Their purpose is to please the eye. They are valued for their beauty. The flashes of blue, yellow, pink, green, and red excite and intrigue. Common opals, Fire Opals, Black Opals of Australia—no two are alike, their differences often detectable by the naked eye.

Mercury is a fluid stone (or mineral) used not only in thermometers, but it can also be used to gather gold flecks and nuggets to be melted into a single button. Its value is in its versatility.

Two stones are particularly pleasing to the imagination. Jasper is composed of various minerals that give it a colorful landscape-like appearance. One can imagine rolling hills, rising mountains, and flowing streams in its patterns. Moss agates have formations that can be perceived as forest scenes, lakes and islands, or jungle pictures. The moss ranges in color from bright green to shades of brown and nearly black. Jasper and moss agates trick the eye and stimulate the imagination.

Turquoise is eye catching. Although it is not considered a precious gem, the colorful blue-green shades quickly grab one's attention. The flamboyance created by combining large stones and silver settings lend a bold ornamental effect.

Diamonds symbolize enduring love and commitment. Their strength is valued in industry as well as in love. Their clear facets reflect light as does no other gem. Diamonds are coveted by women while men risk financial welfare and rejection to provide them for the women they love. They are the ultimate precious gem.

Folks are like rocks. Diverse in their characteristics, they are each to be valued for their individuality. Some are colorful and showy—pleasing to the eye. Others lend their talents to beautify others, thus increasing their own value. Still others require one to look deep into them before discovering their true worth. However, those valued most highly are dependable and strong. They endure time, remaining true and clear. As they reflect the beauty and value in others, they become ever more appealing.

How to Pan for Gold

There are certain life skills that, when mastered, lend great insight into other facets of one's life. So it is with gold prospecting. Only the very hopeful, the very focused, the very persistent will gain the treasure.

Step One: Have a Dream

This is not in reference to the dream that appears in the night identifying the actual location of gold; however, that would be very convenient. Rather it is the dream that one has in his heart of finding treasure, a hope of a reward, a goal.

Step Two: Obtain a Gold Pan

As with any quest, it is important to be prepared with proper equipment. In this case one needs to be in possession of a gold pan. This is a pan used for finding gold, not an actual pan that is gold. Gold pans come in various sizes and can be formed of hard rubber or, as the originals, made of steel. Gold pans appear as oversized pie pans with extended sides. Steel gold pans are preferred as they often rust, giving the appearance of having been used, hopefully by one who has actually experienced success!

Step Three: Find a Mountain Stream

Gold is often hidden at the bottom of a stream or river in a mountain range. This is due to its density, thus allowing it to gravitate as it is washed from the mountainside. It is good to look where gold has been reported to have been found previously. One would not look for prickly pear cactus in Alaska, nor should he pan for gold in the Mojave Desert.

Step Four: Adopt Panning Position

This is done by squatting near a stream enabling one to dip the gold pan deep into the stream bed. It may be convenient to wear some type of wading boot, thus allowing one to venture farther into the middle of the stream. It is advisable to engage in some sort of prior strength training program as this squatting position will quickly become tiring.

Step Five: Begin Panning

Grasp gold pan between both hands, hollowed center facing upwards. With pan tilted at a forty-five degree angle, highest point near one's waist, reach deep into the stream bed and scoop a generous portion of soil into pan. Retain a fair amount of water in the pan as it will be used in the panning process. Pan, soil, and water will be heavy.

Step Six: Begin Swishing Motion

Lower the angle of the pan and begin swishing the water and soil in either a circular or left-right, left-right motion. This process allows heavier materials to be worked to the bottom of the pan while lighter less desirable soil is brought to the surface and can then be washed away. Be certain to maintain some angle on the pan allowing the heavier materials to gather in the elbow or crease between bottom and side of pan. Do not become too energetic, especially as this process takes some time to complete. Vigorous swishing and splashing may result in the washing away of treasure and precipitate fatigue.

Step Seven: Wash Away Unwanted Materials

As the finer soil is accumulated in the water, allow the water to splash over the outer edge of pan and wash away. Gather more water from stream and continue the swishing process.

Step Eight: Obtain Bucket and Stool

Having exhausted one's thighs in squatting position, it is advisable to take a break and obtain a bucket of water and a stool. This will allow prospector to sit while panning. Use the bucket of water for swishing and washing. If neither of these items is available, one might engage a rock or stream bank as substitute for a stool and continue washing into the stream.

Step Nine: Continue Scooping, Swishing, Washing

Step Ten: Exercise Patience

Good things come to those who wait. Did someone famous say that?

Step Eleven: Experience Progress

As the lighter less desirable soils are washed away, darker richer soil appears. However, it too must be discarded as the heavier gold flecks and nuggets lie beneath. This soil is more difficult to clear away as it is similar in characteristics to gold; however, it is in one's way and must be removed as it is separating him from his goal.

Step Twelve: Proceed Carefully

The darker soil must be removed more gently, as too much motion may result in washing away the treasure. Just as a surgeon begins with a larger incision and makes more delicate maneuvers, or as an artist begins with a base coat and continues until fine details complete the work, the prospector must be patient and meticulous as he nears his goal.

Step Thirteen: Gain Hope

The treasure that has been hidden for so long begins to show itself. One will catch glimpses of yellow as he continues to scoop water, swish, and wash. This will be very exciting as he can see that the goal is in sight. He will be encouraged to continue his quest.

Step Fourteen: Rejoice!

Having exercised much diligence and painstaking technique, the prospector will eventually be rewarded. As with any goal, the key to achievement is in the process. Refusing to abandon a plan that has been proven will lead to victory. Treasure found!

Step Fifteen: Begin Again

That's right, one has contracted *Gold Fever*. Success creates a desire for more success. Set another goal. Find another treasure. It will require perseverance. However, if one will stick to the plan he may attain yet another triumph.

No More Boat

That's right—I think it's time to sell the boat. Hopefully, this can be accomplished before it really does sink, as it would be most difficult to market a boat resting on the bottom of the lake! These are the indications that boat ownership has had its day:

The family is outgrowing the load capacity. This is not only due to maturing boys, but we recently acquired a son-in-law. An additional body, life jacket, and water ski heaped upon the ever growing pile of water toys and safety gear makes for a crowded cruise.

My pride is suffering. My swimsuit has lost its elasticity. This would not be an obstacle if I were more agreeable to the public humiliation that occurs when *shopping* for a new suit. They are out there, the ones that make middle aged women look good, but *paying* for them is akin to swamped boat recovery—extremely expensive! Swimsuit shopping could comprise another chapter! The kids, whom we so dutifully tutored in the finer points of skiing, have become better skiers than their parents. Display of my own abilities is increasingly short-lived due to lack of endurance resulting from continued aging. The boot on my twenty-one-year-old ski is tearing out and I am *afraid* of failure on a newer model.

Fuel. Need I say more?

The marriage is suffering! Boat trips increase the levels of stress experienced by the adults responsible for providing recreational opportunities. In other words, we might get along better if we took up knitting or chess. Bailing water causes back problems and I blame my back problems on my husband. Not without merit, mind you. He's the one that didn't screw the plug in tightly! That's why he almost lost his index finger when he had to plug the hole while I bailed as the bilge pump slowly emptied the hull. Good thing he replaced that broken bilge pump! We failed to heed our own counsel—keep spare boat plug in glove box!

If he had lost his finger I may have had more difficulty reading the sign language he sends me—it isn't vulgar, just lots of arm waving—when I'm driving and he's failing to ski. But that happened before he plugged the hole. It was definitely *not* plugged when we took on those gallons and gallons of lake water, full throttle, boat creeping, skiers dragging, arms waving, ten miles upriver!

"Everybody, get your life jackets on!" Only children under age sixteen are required to wear them while in a boat. We had visions of exhausted bodies attempting to swim ten miles to safety having escaped a drowning boat. Kevin made a hard right turn to shore. That's when the plugging and bailing began.

It's convenient to be a kid. One is allowed to keep his head while Mom and Dad will most certainly lose theirs. Panic set in as Brock and his friend (who always happens to be present when boating trauma occurs) took to shore and explored the area. Bail. Bail. Cuss. Cuss. Pray! Our seventeen-year-old resourcefully used a car key to dissect a beach towel and fashion a makeshift boat plug. We inserted—shoved, poked, and smashed the new plug and desperately headed down river to safety.

It never should have worked! Our leisurely outing come tragedy ended safely, fabric plug intact. Nerves shot, we made a bee-line for home and promptly purchased two new boat plugs that remain somewhere in a shopping bag in Wal-Mart. Not to be discouraged, we obtained another pair of boat plugs—one for the boat and one for the glove box. They are resting on my kitchen counter. We haven't been boating since!

Yup, I think it's time to sell the boat.

CHAPTER FIVE

The Later Years

My Search for Mr. Right

The search for Mr. Right has long been a challenge for the All American Girl. I should know. It was a long challenge for me! Few have searched as low and high as I searched. If he stood between 5'0" and 6'10," I checked him out. If he had hair to his shoulders or no hair at all, I checked him out. Young or old, rich or poor, I checked him out. I hunted. I was not without my priorities. I drew the line at *Farmer*. There are some things a girl just shouldn't have to deal with. They are: cow manure, irrigation boots, and lack of proximity to a department store.

In my search for Mr. Right, and my avoidance of farmers, I found a few other things a girl shouldn't have to deal with. They are as follows:

Coupons! I once dated a young man that must have had his first dollar, as well as, his father's first dollar! Okay, that is an exaggeration. He did spend. He owned a very nice little pickup truck and a shotgun. It was his dates that were cheap! I quote, "Do you want to go to lunch? We have to go here, here, or there, and you have to eat this or that, or share one of these. Oh, and since you work so close, could you just meet me there?" It didn't take long for me to feel less than special with *The Coupon Man.*

Pretty Boys! You know the type. I knew I was headed in the wrong direction when my date took longer to dress for a movie than me. His wardrobe filled his living room and his library filled a wastebasket. The day we both showed up with the same hairdo and he looked prettier than I looked, it was over!

Tests! How can a girl pass a test if she doesn't know she is taking one? I dated a fellow that put me in such stressful situations that I couldn't even enjoy the time we spent together. The worst was the time he invited me to dinner at his sister's prefaced with, "Julie is very particular. She likes things nice. She likes things nicer than I do, but you don't need to be nervous." I didn't think I *was* nervous until I snorted my beverage up my nose—and out! That relationship didn't last much longer, and just in time. At least my nerves were salvaged. It was too late for my pride.

There were others—the musician that took me to the symphony and I slept through it—twice. The scholar whose language was so heavy that I had to carry Webster's Dictionary when we went out, and the really, really, nice guys that hung around like mosquitoes.

One day Mr. Right showed up. He took me to a movie and bought me my own bag of popcorn. He wore a cowlick in his unkempt hair and his sneakers had an air vent created by his protruding big toe. He took me rafting and fell in the river all day long. I think he may have snorted some of it up his nose! He couldn't hang around like a mosquito because he always had to get home—to feed and milk his cows. Yup, Mr. Right was a farmer complete with cow manure, irrigation boots, and a JC Penney mail order catalogue! There are some things a girl just has to learn to deal with.

Let the Games Begin

One would believe if one listened to women, that childbirth is a competitive sport! Birthing events range from sprint to marathon and weight lifting to gymnastics. Medals and awards come in the form of bragging rights for the duration of a mother's natural life. No sport has ever been, or ever will be sensationalized as is childbirth when a group of mothers gather together. Medals are worn with honor at all family gatherings, social events, and religious functions. Nary a phone-call occurs between two mothers without reference to and often play-by-play recall of a birthing event. The beauty of the sport lies in that *all* event participants are winners. No birthing experience can be overshadowed by the next, nor is it insignificant compared to those that have gone before. Each is unique displaying beauty and grace, endurance and pain all its own. It is the mothers that supply the competition! Let us examine the events:

The Birthing Sprint. The winner of this event delivered her babies in taxi cabs, motor homes, and hospital elevators. The sheer speed of her labor strikes fear, envy, and disbelief in the hearts of mothers entering into more controlled birthing events. Her bragging rights? It *hurts* to have a baby that fast!

The Birthing Marathon. This mother's labor lasted longer than Van Winkle's nap! Her recounting has an underlying attitude of "Wimp!" towards birthing sprinters. Anyone can hold out for three hours. Three days? Just try that!

The Birthing Weight Lifter. You guessed it, her baby outweighed her suitcase. The strength it required to carry that child for nine months is medal worthy. Deliver a baby that size and even men will grimace in pain.

The Tri-athlete. This competitive spirit delivered a baby, attended a baseball game, and baked a birthday cake for her two-year-old all in a twenty-four hour period. Giving birth is all in a day's work.

The Gymnast. This mother delivers her babies with the aid

of various apparatus, such as: in a hot tub, on a kitchen table, and to the rhythms of Tchaikovsky and Lennon. Variety is the key to her success.

Myself? I'm one who wears the marks of the competition with pride, much as an athlete sports a tattoo of his mascot or Olympic Rings. Grateful to have been invited to participate, I needed the help of a surgeon to complete the event. Even my aided delivery has its bragging rights.

> *Now, I don't mean to brag and I don't mean to boast,*
> *But I have an incision that goes from Coast to Coast.*
> *Hipbone to hipbone, that's the size for me.*
> *The nurses all exclaimed, "Hey, that's a big smilie!"*

My personal favorite is the Creative Dance Participant. This mother was caught in a flood in Mozambique. She delivered her baby while taking refuge in a tree! Try to top that!

The beauty of childbirth competition is that each participant has an experience all her own. It matters not what the competition has done, her experience of sacrifice cements a bond between mother and child none can discount. A memory none can erase. She can't be disqualified or penalized. There is no such thing as a false start. Each emerges victorious. Imply that a mother had an *ordinary* birthing experience and she will launch a colorful recounting that will make the Boston Marathon sound like a walk in the park!

Like Son, Like Father

The very traits that bother us most in our children are often the same habits we recognize in ourselves, such as, nail biting, lip smacking, shifting of blame to inanimate objects …

My husband, Kevin, had been nursing along a weeping beech tree that was failing to thrive, when he discovered one day that it was broken off close to the ground. He was confident the culprit was our precocious four-year-old. Upon interrogation the suspect denied any and all involvement.

"Brock, what happened to my tree?" Kevin was met with an extremely innocent stare. "Do you know who broke my tree?" More staring. This time the feigned innocence was accompanied with a look of confusion. Kevin was even more convinced that the culprit was indeed the three-foot-tall blonde he was questioning. Failing to obtain the confession, he gave up. The tree hadn't been expected to survive and the interview wasn't going well either.

A short time later I exercised my finer skills of interrogation, "I wonder how that tree got broken?"

Brock pointed a tiny finger and confided, "I just touched it, like this, and it fell over!"

"So, you saw it fall over?"

"I just touched it," pointing one tiny finger, "and it fell over." Thus, I obtained the elusive confession.

A few days later, Kevin was eating macaroni salad when he sheepishly produced a gold crown from inside his very expensive mouth.

"How did that come off?" I accused.

He produced an innocent stare and confided, "This noodle sucked it off!"

"Yeah, right, and Brock just touched that tree and it fell over." Like son, like father!

CHAPTER SIX

Mom and Pa-isms

Always Go Home with the Guy What Brung Ya...

Esther had a fine command of the English language; however, she also knew that sometimes communication is more effective when delivered in an incorrect fashion. Whenever Mom uttered such a sentence, she received our attention, as it was uncharacteristic of her to speak in such a casual manner. So it was that she taught her children how to conduct themselves.

Always go home with the guy what brung ya. "The guy what brung me where?" one might ask. And to whose home should I go? "Guys" were "brunging" me places long before I dated, but Esther didn't wait for her children to start dating to teach them this basic principle.

In my youth I assumed that my folks wanted to know where I was, who I was with, and how I was returning home. If I left my home with a particular party, they expected that I would return with the same. It applied both ways. I knew that if I were the driver to any given activity, I was expected to deliver my friends to the location from whence I acquired them. It often distressed me if one of my *charges* decided to forgo my offer of conveyance and take an alternate route. Although this is a critical part of the lesson, it is not the entire lesson.

Always go home. Return to the place you belong. Examine those things that are important. When I was single, living several hours away from the home of my youth, I would often feel the urge to visit my parents for a few days. I would pack up my economy car with enough items for the weekend and my week's worth of laundry and head home. The voyage itself offered time for reflection. As I neared my old stomping grounds I felt a redefining of myself—a remembrance of whom I was. This was especially helpful when recovering from a broken heart! I would eat my mother's cooking, use my mother's laundry soap, move my father's bait box (He had a habit of positioning it by the front door), and pet the family cat. On Monday morning I would be back at work, renewed and determined.

When an individual feels adrift, confused, or unhappy, it is often helpful to *go home*. Revisit those things that have long been most important. If he has moved away from his defining stomping grounds such as family, friends, religious beliefs, hobbies, or moral standards, that examination may shed light on the source of his frustration. Embracing those stomping grounds may bring him to a place, physical or emotional, of safety.

Who is *The Guy*? Whomever. *The Guy* is often the driver of the car, the person that arranged a ride, and sometimes *The Guy* is actually a beau. In a very literal sense, it is wise and respectful to return from an activity with the individual that invited you. Unless one is placed in harm's way, it is only right and proper to devote his time and attention to his host. The party may be dull, the date may be unpleasant, a better offer might come along, but one can live through the inconvenience to maintain his integrity. If the offer is actually better, it will come along again.

Respect *The Guy*. Do unto others. Show your comrades the same consideration you would desire for yourself. I am reminded of a piece of advice given to an acquaintance when she had received an offer of a new job. The new employer wanted her to begin as soon as possible. She was so excited that she was willing to quit her present job immediately so as to please her new boss. The counsel given was this—Give your current employer the regular two weeks notice. It will give him an opportunity to fill your position and show him the respect he deserves. It will also communicate to the new employer that you are an individual that honors your commitments. If you are willing to leave your current job without notice, you would be inclined to do it again. Respecting *The Guy* is simply an exercise in honoring one's commitments.

Brung me where? Physically *bringing* (If I continue to say "brunging" I will never get published!) a body can be anywhere. Someone has helped you. Whether a ride to church, a date to dinner, a lift to school, somebody was instrumental in getting you where you needed to go. It is wise to be grateful for that help.

Where else might one have been brought? While physical *bringing* and the acknowledgement of that help is important, emotional and spiritual *bringing* is still greater. One is often brought to a greater level of understanding, or a more mature and responsible state of being. How often does one find help and strength from a friend? Whether wallowing in depression, or just having a bad hair day, others often reach out to alleviate our pain. Do we express our gratitude? When our pretty good life experiences trial, do we abandon those things that have made that life pretty good in expectation of greener grass, or do we remain loyal to the people and practices that got us there? It is rare that one experiences growth without the aid of another who has gone before.

Always go home with the guy what brung ya. Return to

those things that are valuable, constant, and true. Be respectful of your associates. Appreciate growth and honor those who help you attain that growth. Was it a parent, a sibling, a teacher, a friend, the Savior? Who brung ya, and where did you go?

To Forbid is to Motivate

My children will not eat anything that looks new, smells different, or hasn't remained a staple since they were in diapers. My children are teenagers. I, on the other hand, will try to eat all foods that can't outrun me. I learned this from my father.

Dad didn't attempt to shame us into eating our dinner by claiming, "There are fifty billion starving children in the world," or by giving ultimatums such as, "If you don't eat it, I'll feed it to you!" He simply stated, "You can't have this. This isn't for kids." Sardines were not for kids. I love sardines! Mushrooms, asparagus, seafood of any kind, and cherry chocolates were not for kids.

My father understood a basic rule of parenting—Tell them they can't, and they often will. Dad could get us to eat almost anything. I ate fried oysters, because they were not for kids. I have since determined that fried oysters probably aren't for people, and I don't have to eat them! But as a child, the motivation worked.

The fact is most folks will rise to a challenge, whether that challenge is positive in nature or negative. Tell a ten-year-old that he must go to bed at a given time, and he will do his best to delay. Forbid a teenage girl to see a certain young man, and she is likely to defy the directive. Bet someone they can't hit you with a snowball, and you will often end up with a wet face!

On the other hand, permission granted often dissipates desire. "Dad, can I jump off the house?" "Sure, if you want to break your neck." The desire to jump off the house is overshadowed by the need to keep ones' neck intact. "Mom, do I *have* to go to the dance with *him*?" "No, Dear, you don't *have* to go with him. You can call and break the date if you want folks to believe you don't keep your word." The discomfort of attending a dance with someone undesirable is overshadowed by a need to be respected.

Most people, young or old, simply want to be in charge of their own actions. As a parent, having more information at your disposal is the key to using the forbidding technique. For instance, rather than moan and groan about a child leaving home for kindergarten or preschool, a parent may pave the way by telling the child how much fun she will have at school, making new friends, learning songs, and attending recess. Then when the child misbehaves, the parent can threaten to keep her home another year! The child wants to go to school and play with her friends. Two things will happen—she will strive to be more obedient, and her apprehension regarding school will be alleviated. After all, school is fun.

More power at a one's disposal is also helpful. Try this one with a teenager. "If you don't raise your grades, you won't be driving that car I'm paying for." The desire to be in charge of one's own transportation will quickly motivate the student to work harder to succeed in school. The key, however, is for the parent to be willing to follow through. Although inconvenient, he may have to run his own errands for a time, but watch how quickly the grades improve!

One must be alert while developing this technique. In his efforts to manipulate his children into choosing exactly that which he would himself choose for the child, it is important not to get confused as to when to forbid and when to grant permission. Avoid situations such as, "Dad, would you like me to mow the lawn?" "Absolutely not!" This is a little extreme. Child will gladly escape before parent can correct error. Or, "Mom, can I eat the rest of the ice cream?" "Go ahead. I don't care if you get fat." Child doesn't care either. Ice cream will disappear.

It is most important to be aware of others' attempts to perfect the forbidding technique. Do not get caught in the same web. For instance, when a child insists he can clean the kitchen by himself, yet takes upwards of an hour to do the dishes, he is simply trying to obtain assistance or get relieved of the responsibility altogether. If one falls for this manipulation, he'll never get that Sunday nap that he so badly needs!

Moral: That which is most out of reach is most sought after.

Oh, About So . . .

It has been told that Grandma Nelson, the Miner's mother, could make a meal out of nothing. It was like magic. One would inspect her icebox and cupboards concluding that there was, in fact, nothing to eat and in what seemed no time at all, Viola Agnes Thompson Nelson would produce a fine spread. Incredibly, not only did she pass this talent on to her children, but she must have passed it to her children's spouses as well, for you see, Esther possessed the same magical talent.

One cookbook and a drawer full of miscellaneous recipes were all the formal directions Esther owned. She seldom used them. Rather, Esther cooked *out of her head*. I recall the day she determined to teach me how to make bread. "Put some warm water and yeast in a big bowl."

"How much water?" I asked.

"Oh, about so . . ."

"How warm should the water be?"

She splashed her hand in the bowl and said "Oh, about like this ..." I felt the water and determined that I wasn't sure how warm it was. Not too hot. Not too cool.

When the yeast began to grow and become rather disgusting, she added some salt and then flour. How much flour? About so. Esther began to work the flour into a sponge, adding a pat of butter here and a pat of butter there until she had a batch of bread dough. Later, she punched down the dough and formed it into four loaves. These were placed in a 9 x 13 inch baking pan, allowed to rise and then baked to perfection. The best parts were the four adjoining corners that pulled apart, just right for taste testing. Often, the corners became scooped out by overzealous testers!

A chicken or turkey carcass that appeared fit only for the family cat quickly became noodle soup or chicken and dumplings. Open a jar of pickles, add some bread and homemade jam, slice a tomato or two, and one has a complete meal.

Some of her greatest creations involved an iron skillet. Amazing, the dishes that can be concocted in an iron skillet! Topping the list were fried chicken and fried trout. The bottom? Fried oysters. (See *To Forbid is to Motivate*) The middle of the list is lengthy, as well as, tasty. Esther could produce a very large breakfast using only one skillet. This is how it was done.

Obtain several slices of bacon and fry them until crispy. Remove bacon, reserving *some* of the grease in the pan while saving *a bit* for later use. Take three small trout and coat them in flour that has been seasoned with, oh, about so much salt and pepper. Place in frying pan with reserved grease and fry until tender. Remove trout and place on platter with bacon. Place in oven to keep warm. Throw *a few* onion slices and *some* grated baked potato into the pan. Add additional bacon grease as needed. Cook until crisp. Remove potatoes and onion to warming platter. Get six baking powder biscuits from bread drawer and add them to the warming platter. Add more grease to skillet. Crack four eggs and scramble with a dab of milk and a dash of salt and pepper. Serve entire meal with butter, jam, salt and pepper. (Just a note: Although this diet seems ripe for a coronary attack, it has served a long line of octogenarians remarkably well.)

Pork chops, milk gravy, fried squash, pancakes, French toast, and caramelized sugar for flavoring Burnt Sugar Cake were among the many delectables Esther whipped up with her iron skillet. The more she used it, the better it cooked. The more she cooked, the less she opened a cookbook. When transcribing recipe instructions it was important to decipher the meaning of, *about so, just a bit,* and *some*. I learned that those terms meant it really doesn't matter if you get it just right or not. The best test is taste.

There are legacies passed from one generation to the next. Many take planning and purpose, others just happen. While I prefer a bread machine, I can make chicken noodle soup from a carcass. I open my cookbooks for baking recipes, but seldom for main dishes. And I own a well-used, well-loved iron skillet.

When my daughter left for college she packed a very heavy Dutch oven. She called recently to ask, "When do I put the flour in the stew?" I replied, "Oh, before you brown the meat ... or after." And as she was asking how much flour to use, I thought to myself, "Oh, about so ..."

Now, That's a Baby

What mother in an attempt to teach her children good manners hasn't offered the advice, "If you can't say something nice, don't say anything at all"? This rule has been drilled into children for generations. It is difficult to learn. Not because children are inherently mean, but because they are, at the same time, trying very hard to learn to be honest. Occasionally, honesty and nicety are contradictory! How confusing is that? Always tell the truth unless, of course, the truth isn't nice, then one shouldn't tell the truth because it wouldn't be nice to tell the truth. Huh? It is those honestly brutal instances in which one would be well-advised to adopt the practice of Wells, "If you can't say something nice, say something else."

Let's face it, not every baby born on this earth is gorgeous. Though their mothers are blinded by love and their Grandmother's believe their own offspring could never produce a child that was less than perfect in every way, every now and then one runs across a baby that just doesn't radiate good looks. He may be angelic, pure of spirit and possessing a pleasing personality, he may be bright and talented, but at first glance a stranger has only one piece of evidence to go on—appearance. One would be well-advised to keep his mouth shut in such circumstances as commenting on the child's looks would either be dishonest, or not nice. That would all be well and good except for the unarguable fact that doting parents and grandparents *expect* a comment when showing off their newborn. What should one do? *Don't* do as my rancher friend and exclaim, "That was a bad cross!" Say something else. Wells would smile and say really quite honestly, "Now, that's a baby!"

Who hasn't had the opportunity to dine at a friend's home, only to be disappointed that the meat was tough, the gravy lumpy, or the vegetables over cooked. While he appreciates the hospitality, he can't honestly comment on the dinner. It wouldn't be nice! Yet, a comment is *expected*. Say something else. Try, "That was quite a meal!" It's truthful and the friend won't be offended. She may, however, invite one to dine again in which case brutal honesty may be preferable.

It is difficult, maintaining one's integrity without offending his neighbor. In an effort to be kind, polite, or politically correct, society has abandoned sincerity. It has become more important to make someone feel good than to be genuine and truthful. It is easier to offer a counterfeit compliment than it is to look one in the eye and come up with legitimate praise. Test it out. Look a friend in the eye while offering false flattery. It is extremely uncomfortable. However, communicating the truth, lovingly, will allow both parties to feel validated.

They are called *True Roommates*. The friends who tell one her slip is showing whether in public or private. Those who wipe the mustard from one's face *before* they introduce him to a business associate aren't pointing out his faults, only helping him present his best self. Spinach caught between the front teeth? That's a job for a *True Roommate*. A *True Roommate* is *expected* to be brutally honest. A *True Roommate* may get her teeth knocked out if she is not forthright. I recall the day I lasted through an hour of church before I noticed the facing was hanging out the back of my blouse. Not a *True Roommate* in the congregation! Not even on my own pew!

Might I offer a word of caution? Casual acquaintances do not want *you* to be a *True Roommate*. They want someone to coo over their newborn. They want you to rave about their cooking and ask for seconds. They want you to be dazzled by their crimson dress, no matter how ill fitting. They desire political correctness. They want everything *nice*. So, when faced with a sticky situation, don't forget to maintain integrity. Be genuine. Think on one's feet. Take a page out of Wells' book, look her in the eye, smile sweetly, and exclaim, "Wow, that's a red dress!"

Keep a Candle Burning

Candles have been used in the modern era mostly for ambiance. I don't recall mood candles during my youth. Mostly, candles were used during power outages, a common occurrence in Southeast Idaho—the wind, you see. It seems it was after I moved away that Esther developed an affinity for candles. (If she had in fact used them previously, I in my self-absorbed teenage existence had not noticed.) Whenever I returned home for a visit, there would be a candle burning, often in my room.

Candles have many uses other than lighting. They are also valuable for mood setting, covering odors of deep fried foods or camouflaging mouse infestations, and message sending.

Message sending. This is not in reference to smoke signals, although a candle may suffice in a pinch. The messages sent by lighted candles are simple unspoken words of love. For me, a candle communicates, "Welcome Home." Never was Esther's lighted candle so appreciated as it was Christmastime 1983.

Bonnie, the Baby, and I were traveling home from Southwest Idaho to Southeast Idaho for Christmas. Young, single, and not very wise nor well-prepared, we were anxious to hurry home for the holidays and left Boise at 5:00 pm in a light snowstorm on December 23. The trouble with light snowstorms in Southwest Idaho is not only Southwestern Idahoans' lack of winter driving experience, but also the fact that the storm's counterpart in Southeast Idaho is most likely a blizzard.

The light snowstorm increased in severity as we traveled eastward. Halfway between our point of departure and our destination, at about 7:30 pm, the storm became so vigorous that the gas line in Bonnie's Mustang began to freeze up. When this phenomenon occurs, the engine behaves as if the fuel tank is empty and the vehicle comes to a stop. Being quite familiar with the behavior of empty gas tanks, I proceeded to berate her for neglecting to fuel the car. She assured me this was not the case and we began to strategize. Hazards on. Wait patiently for help. Surely someone would come to the rescue. One problem. Folks don't like to stop on freeways in blizzards at night. Second problem. Folks have difficulty seeing in blizzards. Third problem. Hazard lights don't last long in blizzards.

The whiteout was severe enough that we could not determine our exact location. Not that it would do any good as this was in the days before cell phones. We waited. Our only hope was to attract attention and communicate the need for help. We began taking turns standing behind the car and waving the only signal item we had, a white grocery bag! We prayed. As the hazard lights were beginning to dim, we prayed some more and gave up on the white flag waving.

We were becoming most discouraged when not one, but two vehicles transporting *Good Samaritans* stopped to lend a hand. We were offered a ride to town, where we enlisted the help of a garage and tow truck. Bonnie then returned to the scene, accompanying the tow truck driver in an attempt to locate our abandoned vehicle. Several hours later the gas line was thawed and we continued our trek across state. As we reentered the freeway, we discovered that the blizzard was continuing to rage. The white out persisted, but we miraculously arrived home about 2:30 am December 24. As we pulled into the drive, I caught sight of a candle still burning in the window. What a relief! Its flickering glow seemed to communicate, "I'm waiting."

Esther's version of the story is quite different as she was the lighter of the candle. She has spoken of the relief experienced when she observed the glow of the Mustang's headlights coming up the road. She saw the lights and knew we were safe.

Now I don't know if those burning candles were used to set a mood, cover up the odor of a seldom used basement, or send a message, but they were a comfort to me. My own children are maturing and have occasion to be away from home. I have taken up the torch, as it were. A lighted candle now burns while I await their safe return. Mood setting? Maybe. Mostly, I burn the candle in remembrance of the relief it granted me, as a connection to my own mother concerned for the safe travel of her offspring, and to foster a tradition that I am certain my children will not fully understand until they have youngsters of their own venturing forth into the world. Maybe they too, will say a prayer and light a candle to beckon, "Welcome Home."

Printed in the United States
129008LV00002B/1-69/P

9 781596 636262